"*Habits of Hope* offers a transformative road map for students and teachers navigating today's challenges. The essays in this book present a vision of education oriented toward the end of communion with God. When interpreted through the lens of Christian hope, the practices of reading, writing, and conversation become habits that cultivate holiness. A great, thought-provoking, and inspiring read for such a time as this."

Edgardo A. Colón-Emeric, Irene and William McCutcheon Professor of Reconciliation and Theology and dean of the Divinity School at Duke University

"During this cultural moment where discord and division dominate the contemporary landscape, it is essential that educators at all levels provide learning experiences that cultivate the virtue of hope in the lives of our students. By drawing on the wisdom of a diverse group of authors, this volume offers judicious insights into a variety of educational practices designed to resist fear and despair and nurture human flourishing. I encourage faculty, administrators, and church educators to engage with this timely text."

Kim S. Phipps, president of Messiah University in Mechanicsburg, Pennsylvania

"In a time of cultural collapse, this collection inspires hope as faithful obedience but also an antidote for a weary age. This hope is not a fleeting wish, but a purposeful, spiritual assurance that can be cultivated in practices for teaching, writing, learning, conversation, and considering the other. In these inspiring habits of hope, we see the vital contribution Christian education might offer the world."

Michael D. Hammond, president of Gordon College in Wenham, Massachusetts

"*Habits of Hope* brilliantly illuminates the transformative power of hope within Christian higher education. With profound insights and practical wisdom, this book serves as a guiding light for educators and leaders, seamlessly integrating hope into their daily work. It not only encourages but empowers individuals to navigate the challenges of our current world with a movement filled with the hope of Christ."

Deanna L. Porterfield, president of Seattle Pacific University

"Hope is not theoretical. It is a practice and a choice. *Habits of Hope* reminds us that while there is real suffering in our world and on our campuses, Christian higher education can and should make the active choice to cultivate hope to honor our relationships with God, one another, and our communities. The diverse authors and insights in this volume provide a pathway to hope for us to follow, inspired by our faith."

Molly A. Schaller, professor of higher education and associate dean of the School of Education at St. Louis University

"Hope can be simultaneously ubiquitous and elusive, familiar and amorphous, profound and cliché, but as the contributors of *Habits of Hope* remind us, real hope is absolutely indispensable in educational contexts. Whether you are encouraging readers to think about hope from biblical, theological, psychological, equitable, or practical perspectives, *Habits of Hope* is required reading for those who see Christian hope and transformative educational outcomes as inseparable."

Beck A. Taylor, president of Samford University in Birmingham, Alabama

"With the myriad threats and challenges facing students and teachers today, the landscape of formal education often feels more life-draining than life-giving. Hope is desperately needed in this space. *Habits of Hope* offers just this, not by introducing new educational techniques or interventions but by sketching a spiritually and theologically rich vision of hope and exploring how we might teach and learn in light of it. This is a stimulating and edifying work."

Jason Baehr, professor of philosophy at Loyola Marymount University in Los Angeles

FOREWORD BY AMOS YONG

HABITS OF HOPE

*Educational Practices
for a Weary World*

TODD C. REAM, JERRY PATTENGALE,
and CHRISTOPHER J. DEVERS, EDS.

Academic
An imprint of InterVarsity Press
Downers Grove, Illinois

InterVarsity Press
P.O. Box 1400 | Downers Grove, IL 60515-1426
ivpress.com | email@ivpress.com

InterVarsity Press® is the publishing division of InterVarsity Christian Fellowship/USA®. For more information, visit intervarsity.org.

All Scripture quotations, unless otherwise indicated, are taken from The Holy Bible, New International Version®, NIV®. Copyright © 1973, 1978, 1984, 2011 by Biblica, Inc.™ Used by permission of Zondervan. All rights reserved worldwide. www.zondervan.com. The "NIV" and "New International Version" are trademarks registered in the United States Patent and Trademark Office by Biblica, Inc.™

While any stories in this book are true, some names and identifying information may have been changed to protect the privacy of individuals.

The publisher cannot verify the accuracy or functionality of website URLs used in this book beyond the date of publication.

Cover design: David Fassett
Interior design: Daniel van Loon
Image: © gregobagel / E+ / Getty Images

ISBN 978-1-5140-1070-9 (hardcover) | ISBN 978-1-5140-1069-3 (print) | ISBN 978-1-5140-1071-6 (digital)

Printed in the United States of America ∞

Library of Congress Cataloging-in-Publication Data
Names: Ream, Todd C., editor. | Pattengale, Jerry A., editor. | Devers,
    Christopher J., 1977- editor.
Title: Habits of hope : educational practices for a weary world / Todd C.
    Ream, Jerry Pattengale, and Christopher J. Devers ; foreword by Amos
    Yong.
Description: Downers Grove, IL : IVP Academic, [2024] | Includes
    bibliographical references and index.
Identifiers: LCCN 2024021119 (print) | LCCN 2024021120 (ebook) | ISBN
    9781514010693 (print) | ISBN 9781514010709 (cloth) | ISBN 9781514010716
    (digital)
Subjects: LCSH: Education–Religious aspects–Christianity. | Church and
    education. | Hope–Religious aspects–Christianity. |
    Education–Philosophy. | Christian education–United States. | BISAC:
    EDUCATION / Philosophy, Theory & Social Aspects | RELIGION / Christian
    Education / General
Classification: LCC LB1027.223 .H33 2024 (print) | LCC LB1027.223 (ebook)
    | DDC 268–dc23/eng/20240609
LC record available at https://lccn.loc.gov/2024021119
LC ebook record available at https://lccn.loc.gov/2024021120

31 30 29 28 27 26 25 24 | 13 12 11 10 9 8 7 6 5 4 3 2 1

"The days are coming," declares the Sovereign LORD,

"when I will send a famine through the land—

not a famine of food or a thirst for water,

but a famine of hearing the words of the LORD.

People will stagger from sea to sea

and wander from north to east,

searching for the word of the LORD,

but they will not find it."

Amos 8:11-12 NIV

CONTENTS

FOREWORD

Amos Yong

CHRISTIAN EDUCATION GOES BACK, arguably, to when those who were filled with the Holy Spirit on the day of Pentecost thereafter gathered from day to day and "devoted themselves to the apostles' teaching and fellowship, to the breaking of bread and the prayers" (Acts 2:42, NRSVUE throughout). According to the Greek-writing author of the Pentecost narrative, this community of believers committed themselves to the apostolic *didache*—teaching of doctrine—in accordance with the overarching purpose of the Spirit's infilling activity: to enable and commission them as "witnesses in Jerusalem, in all Judea and Samaria, and to the ends of the earth" (Acts 1:8). These words of Jesus outlined their evangelistic vocation and its gradual expansion across the lifespan of the first generation.

And yet, this evangelical propagation of the good news of Jesus Christ also unfolded amid a Mediterranean world weary of imperial Roman rule, a struggle captured by an ancient prophetic text that was drawn on to explicate the meaning of the Pentecost event to the crowd gathered there:

> This is what was spoken through the prophet Joel:
> "In the last days it will be, God declares,
>   that I will pour out my Spirit upon all flesh,
>   and your sons and your daughters shall prophesy. . . .
> And I will show portents in the heaven above
>   and signs on the earth below,
>   blood, and fire, and smoky mist.
> The sun shall be turned to darkness

and the moon to blood,
  before the coming of the Lord's great and glorious day.
  Then everyone who calls on the name of the Lord shall be saved."
  (Acts 2:16-17, 19-21)

These were apocalyptic times, indeed, times for which the promise of divine salvation rang out the hope urgently needed for a world beset by fears of all that was unraveling.

Rarely do books on Christian education, much less Christian higher education, foreground the hopes that motivate and undergird our educational initiatives and activities. *Habits of Hope* thus arrives as fresh air on the scene, probing the affective underpinnings of what galvanizes our efforts as educators. It is, after all, the aspirations, desires, and overarching *teloi* or goals and purposes of education—effectively, our hopes and dreams for such—that fortify our perseverance in these tasks.

Education is an investment in our future/s, and even more pointedly, in that of those we love most dearly: our children (and their generation) and also—here now writing as one whose adult children have given my wife and me six additional little lives so far!—our grandchildren (and their generation). Thus, we are hitting very close to home: we educate those coming after us so they can experience a fuller and perhaps even create a better life and world than the one we now (hopefully!) enjoy, with all its problems and ills.

And, in our day and time, while we may educate in order to pass on the best aspects of the good life to the next generation, including but not limited to the beholding of beauty, the pursuit of truth, and formation of virtue and goodness in our personal lives, we undertake this task also beset on every side, whether by political turmoil, social upheaval, economic turbulence, or climate change that we confront with all our fellow human beings. When put in these ways, we can see how our educational endeavors may be activated by the yearnings we have for the future of our species even as we also realize such are driven at least implicitly by our fears of how to ameliorate the challenges we confront. One of our essayists in the pages to follow lays out clearly how societal worries about educational trends and even our culture wars are fueled by fears, even as another draws on Aquinas to point out that there is a correlation between our hopes and our fears, with the former oftentimes deriving impetus from the spoken and unspoken perceptions of the latter.

And yes, *Habits of Hope* recognizes the perils of our age but refuses to dwell on such due especially to the Christian hope that fuels our lives. Applied educationally, then, the contributors to this book lift up the kinds of practices that, when forged Christianly and hopefully, provide the bedrock on which the next generation is formed and shaped for the difficult issues that they will have to navigate. Thereby, habits of conversing (listening and speaking), of reading, of writing, of including difference, and of teaching, among others, are elaborated on, which are the primary practices through which learning happens in the here and now, even as we believe they will equip and resource Christian faithfulness amid our wariness regarding the future.

The chapters to come are effective pedagogically in highlighting how hopefulness fuels these more mundane educational activities today. Christian hope is most powerfully embodied, then, not because we live in the future but because we are focused in the present moment on practicing hopeful habits related to the shaping of minds, hearts, and hands for life and in all of its complexities.

Before handing you, the reader, on to the rest of the book, I want to return to the Pentecost motif with which I began, now to emphasize in other words what the author of the chapter "Inclusive Excellence: Diversity as a Hopeful Educational Practice" so crucially named: that the Spirit's initial inspiration of apostolic teaching was expressed in the native or indigenous languages—the mother tongues, so to speak—of those gathered from every nation under heaven (Acts 2:5-6). "In our own languages we hear them speaking about God's deeds of power" (Acts 2:11), said the crowd, which explains also why amid amazement and astonishment there was perplexity and bewilderment: "What does this mean?" they also asked (Acts 2:12).

Education happens at least in part through dissonance, and the latter is facilitated by encountering otherness. The Pentecost narrative lifts up the many tongues of those from many peoples, nations, and tribes. In our educational contexts today, these happen most organically when there are many voices—linguistically, ethnically/racially, culturally, sociopolitically, disciplinarily, ideologically, and so on—gathered around the classroom conversation tables (whether in person or on e-learning platforms), included in our syllabi and reading lists, encouraged in our writing genres (as the chapter on this topic so helpfully suggests), and experimented with in our teaching styles, strategies, and repertoires. I am hopeful that those who attend carefully to the rest of this volume will find the pedagogical and educational pluralism developed to be empowering even when, as it inevitably and regularly happens, we find ourselves weary of continuing to do this work.

AN EXPECTATION OF THE WORLD TO COME

Todd C. Ream, Jerry Pattengale,
and Christopher J. Devers

*Remember that hope is a good thing, Red, maybe the
best of things, and no good thing ever dies.*

Andy Dufresne to Ellis Boyd Redding, in
Rita Hayworth and Shawshank Redemption, by Stephen King

Perhaps unbeknownst to one another, the editors of *The Hedgehog Review* and *Plough* offered their audience members beleaguered by a mix of COVID-19 and political fragmentation theme issues in 2022 titled, respectively, "Hope Itself" and "Hope in Apocalypse." When closing his editorial note for the fall issue, *The Hedgehog Review*'s Jay Tolson offered, "Hope may be the most demanding virtue—and, in our time, the one in greatest need."[1]

As the title he selected suggests, *Plough*'s Peter Mommsen led his readers into a seemingly counter-instinctual space—one in which thoughts of the apocalypse and hope are not only related but even

---

[1]Jay Tolson, "From the Editor," *The Hedgehog Review* 24, no. 3 (2022): 8.

inextricable. When closing his editorial note for the summer issue, Mommsen contended:

> The resurrected Jesus—a flesh-and-blood person who in the Gospels eats a meal, breaks bread, and roasts fish at a lakeside campfire—is proof and pioneer of what humankind will be. . . . In the interim of the ages, as the universe's great Sabbath approaches, humankind has work to do. Plant the sapling; tend the earthworms; welcome the children given to you; hope. The times may be troubled but beyond them, there's a future to eagerly await.[2]

However difficult to comprehend, the significance of Mommsen's words concerning how to understand hope and live accordingly should prove compelling to all of us. When it comes to the cultivation of the virtue of hope, our expectation of the end of time narrates how we live in the present.

Although many possible observations that come from Mommsen's words merit unpacking, two prove most noteworthy. First, hope is inextricably tied to our anticipation of the world to come—a world inaugurated by the life, death, and resurrection of Jesus Christ. In essence, the character hope presently summons falls short of what God intends when disconnected from an expectation of the world to come.[3]

Second, the character hope summons is not passive but active in nature. "Humankind has work to do," and that work in the world at hand is given purpose and order when conducted in the light offered by the expectation of the world to come.

This book extends that theological logic concerning hope to the work humans called to the academic vocation do. The disorientation plaguing individuals called to such a vocation was on the rise through the 2010s, with COVID-19 only exacerbating it.[4] Although the pandemic has

---

2Peter Mommsen, "From the Editor," *Plough* 32 (2022): 21.
3One of the most eloquent articulations of the connection between hope and the apocalypse is offered by Judith Wolfe in her chapter "Hope," in *The Edinburgh Critical History of Twentieth Century Christian Theology*, ed. Philip G. Ziegler (Edinburgh: Edinburgh University Press, 2022), 333-44.
4For example, please note articles such as Colleen Flaherty's "Trashing Morale," *Inside Higher Ed*, November 17, 2014, www.insidehighered.com/news/2014/11/18/should-faculty-members-have -take-out-their-own-trash.

gratefully eased, that sense of disorientation is one from which educators have yet to recover.[5]

In an effort to address the challenge facing individuals called to the Christian academic vocation, this volume focuses on:

1. building upon an understanding that an expectation of the world to come is the proper theological context in which to cultivate the virtue of hope in the world at hand;

2. establishing an understanding of the virtue of hope as being critical to how individuals understand their calling to the Christian academic vocation; and

3. detailing how specific educational practices (integration, conversation, diversity, reading, writing, and teaching) are practices that continue to cultivate the virtue of hope not only within Christian educators but also within the myriad of internal and external constituents those educators are called to serve.

THE HOPE OF CHRISTIAN HUMANISM

To avoid the temptation to collapse into a passive understanding of hope—an understanding that may look more like wishful thinking than one that knows of no distinction between theory and practice—the understanding of hope that defines this work is one drawn from the riches of Christian humanism.

Perhaps the most concise compilation of those riches is found in Joseph M. Shaw, R.W. Franklin, Harris Kaasa, and Charles W. Buzicky's (eds.) *Reading in Christian Humanism* (Fortress Press, 1982). Beginning with a selection by Justin Martyr and concluding with one by Langdon Gilkey, Shaw, Franklin, Kaasa, and Buzicky established the understanding that Christian humanism not only occupies a history far more expansive than its secular alternative but can only be appreciated when theologically contextualized well.[6]

---

[5]For example, please note articles such as Colleen Flaherty's "Calling It Quits," *Inside Higher Ed*, July 4, 2022, www.insidehighered.com/news/2022/07/05/professors-are-leaving-academe-during-great-resignation.

[6]For a history of the secular alternative, please note Sarah Bakewell's *Humanly Possible: Seven Hundred Years of Humanist Free Thinking, Inquiry, and Hope* (New York: Penguin Press, 2023).

Each contributor to this volume taps into the distinct yet expansive understanding Christian humanism affords hope and does so in his or her own way. The most articulate understanding from which contributors draw their understanding of hope, however, is arguably offered by Dominic F. Doyle in *The Promise of Christian Humanism: Thomas Aquinas on Hope* (Herder & Herder, 2011). Although Thomas Aquinas's appeal to Protestants and, in particular, Protestant evangelicals is relatively recent, Thomas's contribution concerning the virtues and, in particular, the theological virtue of hope may prove more valuable to this group of contributors.

Part of the value of Thomas's understanding of hope articulated by Doyle is "by uniting the desire for religious transcendence with a commitment to the present good, hope securely grounds the contemporary renewal of Christian humanism."[7] In relation to our particular purpose, hope securely grounds education and the practices that define it as an expression of Christian humanism—activities defined by the expectation of a world to come but lived out in the world at hand.

Despite the long history that Christian humanism and hope share, no book applies such an understanding of hope (or any understanding of hope for that matter) to how individuals understand their calling to the Christian academic vocation and then cultivate hope through how they exercise various educational practices.

Perhaps the best way to offer an outline of recent titles of a related nature is to begin with Ernst Bloch's *The Principle of Hope*. Originally published in 1954 (and currently published in English by MIT Press in three volumes), Bloch drew upon the work of Hegel and Marx to offer what philosophers often refer to as Bloch's "not-yet consciousness." Such an understanding affords individuals (Bloch's work is often referred to as even being privatized in focus) who encounter challenges that may prove precarious or even tragic with what hope—an anticipation of a greater appreciation of the future and what it means to be human—may offer.

---

[7]Dominic F. Doyle, *The Promise of Christian Humanism: Thomas Aquinas on Hope* (New York: Herder & Herder, 2011), 3.

Inspired by Bloch, perhaps the most prominent theologian to grapple with hope during the twentieth century was Jürgen Moltmann. Risking understatement, Moltmann, a German and Reformed theologian, returned hope to the forefront of theological discourse and the role hope was called to play in Christian discipleship. Originally published in 1965 (and currently published in English by Fortress), Moltmann's *A Theology of Hope* identifies the event of the crucifixion as nothing other than the source of hope for all people who invest their faith in such a sacrifice.

Although Moltmann proved to be one of the most prolific and influential theologians since World War II, his work never wandered far from this theme. For example, in 2019 Moltmann published *The Spirit of Hope: Theology for a World in Peril* (Westminster John Knox). On the eve of COVID-19, Moltmann once again drew attention to a theological logic that draws "Christian hope and the promised future of God into the present day, and prepares the present day for this future."[8] He then discussed the relevance of such a logic to challenges ranging from the state of the natural environment to the presence of nuclear weapons.

Moltmann's Catholic and German contemporary, Josef Pieper, published the landmark *Hope and History* in 1969. Along with Christian humanists such as Jacques Maritain as well as leaders of the *ressourcement* movement, Pieper was among the first to reintroduce the theological logic of Thomas Aquinas and, in this particular case, the value of a theological virtue such as hope. Although hope was less central to Pieper's theological project than to Moltmann's, Pieper also published *On Hope* in German in 1977 (and now published in English by Ignatius Press).

Hope may always find its most prominent place in the literature in theology and philosophy. However, it has also gained a presence in a myriad of disciplines in recent years, including in biology and psychology. One of the most prominent of those titles is Norman Cousins's national bestseller *Head First: The Biology of Hope and the Healing Power of the Human Spirit* (Penguin Press, 1990). Four years later, C. R. Snyder,

---

[8]Jürgen Moltmann, *The Spirit of Hope: Theology for a World in Peril* (Louisville, KY: Westminster John Knox, 2019), 8.

arguably the foremost promoter of what came to be known as positive psychology, published *The Psychology of Hope* (Free Press, 1994).

Some works cross disciplinary lines, such as Adrienne Martin's *How We Hope: A Moral Psychology* (Princeton University Press, 2013), and some works even do so autobiographically, such as Martin E. P. Seligman's *The Hope Circuit: A Psychologist's Journey from Helplessness to Optimism* (PublicAffairs, 2018). Keeping track of the myriad of ways hope has woven its way into various disciplines requires one to consider works such as C. R. Snyder's (ed.) *Handbook of Hope: Theories, Measures, and Applications* (Academic Press, 2000) or Steven C. van den Heuvel's (ed.) *Historical and Multidisciplinary Perspectives on Hope* (Springer, 2020).

Hope's ability to cross disciplinary lines, however, in no way diminished the role it played in philosophy and theology in recent years. In philosophy, for example, Philip E. Wegner published *Invoking Hope: Theory and Utopia in Dark Times* (University of Minnesota Press, 2020) and Michael Lamb published *A Commonwealth of Hope: Augustine's Political Thought* (Princeton University Press, 2022).

In theology, hope is present in a growing number of titles. If making a distinction between academic and popular theology is apt or even wise, one finds a growing number of recent titles on hope present in both groups. In academic theology, for example, one finds works such as David Eliot's *Hope and Christian Ethics* (Cambridge University Press, 2017) and David Newheiser's *Hope in a Secular Age: Deconstruction, Negative Theology, and the Future of Faith* (Cambridge University Press, 2019).

In popular theology, one finds some of the most influential voices contributing works concerning hope, including N. T. Wright in *Surprised by Hope: Rethinking Heaven, the Resurrection, and the Mission of the Church* (HarperOne, 2008), Tim Keller in *Hope in Times of Fear: The Resurrection and the Meaning of Easter* (Hodder & Stoughton, 2021), and Robert Barron in *Renewing Our Hope: Essays for the New Evangelization* (Catholic University of America Press, 2020).

Although hope's presence has grown in volume and in disciplinary reach since the mid-twentieth century, a review of the literature yields no titles in education as defined by this volume. Kevin M. Gannon's *Radical*

Hope: A Teaching Manifesto (West Virginia University Press, 2020) may, in fact, be the only title that draws hope into any conversation concerning education. Part of the purpose of this volume is to fill that void.

Volume Overview

Chapter one is "The Cross Our Hope: The Hope of Education," by Kevin G. Grove, CSC. Stemming from the context set by the introduction, Kevin Grove will offer a theologically expansive understanding of hope and then link that understanding, via Christian humanism, to the value of education and the practices that define it. Grove is a member of the Congregation of Holy Cross, a still relatively young order that emerged in response to "The Terror" unleashed by the French Revolution. Defined by the charisms of parish ministry, education, and missions, the motto of the Congregation of Holy Cross is *Ave Crux, Spes Unica* (Hail the Cross, Our Only Hope). That motto and the sense of hope it fosters has defined the Congregation's efforts for almost two hundred years. Grove thus draws upon the context in which he was called into the ministry as a way of framing his understanding of hope and then points readers to the discussions of the educational practices that follow.

Chapter two is "Past, Present, and Future: Integration as a Hopeful Educational Practice," by Philip Graham Ryken. Integration or, more broadly speaking, the fostering of the relationship shared by faith and learning is, by its very nature, the most hopeful practice a Christian educational institution can offer the internal and external constituents it serves. Those internal constituents include, first and foremost, students who encounter how educators in and beyond the classroom model such a way of viewing the world. Those external constituents include anyone who benefits from the educational programming and materials that educators (and, at times, students) produce, including, for example, articles, concerts, books, and lectures. Among Christian educational institutions, Wheaton College stands as a leader in terms of how it promotes integration. As Wheaton's president, Philip Ryken not only explores how hope informs integration but also offers examples concerning how integration is practiced.

Chapter three is "The Way of Words: Conversation as a Hopeful Educational Practice," by Cherie Harder. Perhaps no educational practice is more in peril today than conversation. For example, speakers whose views are found objectionable for any number of reasons are "shouted down" by audience members. Students, in turn, find themselves incurring diatribes offered by instructors. The challenge, however, is that perhaps no practice is more foundational than the ability of people to gather and discuss their views about a particular topic or question in a disciplined and charitable manner. Such conversations can prove inherently enjoyable, but such conversations can also serve as a means of drawing individuals closer to the truth than isolated reflection may offer. Hope concerning the role of conversations defines the mission of the Trinity Forum. As its president, Cherie Harder convenes conversations concerning a range of topics that model that hope. In her chapter, Harder not only explores the contours of such conversations, but also details why they prove critical to Christian education.

Chapter four is "Inclusive Excellence: Diversity as a Hopeful Educational Practice," by Kimberly Battle-Walters Denu. Despite the significant and widespread role it plays as an educational practice, the theory defining diversity often lags in comparison to other practices.[9] Most educational institutions weave diversity into educational offerings that occur in and beyond the classroom. The rationales educators articulate for diversity are often more reflective of social and/or political thinking than, however, philosophical and theological deliberation. As a result, diversity's role as an educational practice often also garners more controversy than other educational practices. Although Christian educational institutions contend with such controversies, they are also defined by an anthropology (or what it means to be created in God's image) and an ecclesiology (or what it means to be the body of Christ) that offer robust theoretical contexts in which such diversity can be rooted. As Westmont College's provost, Kimberly Battle-Waters Denu describes how she

---

[9]Scholars have sought to address the way diversity theory lags diversity practice since at least the 1990s. For example, see Cynthia Willet, ed., *Theorizing Multiculturalism: A Guide to the Current Debate* (Malden, MA: Wiley-Blackwell, 1998).

develops an appreciation for those roots as well as how she works with the educators she leads to inform educational offerings that occur in and beyond the classroom.

Chapter five is "Reading for Deification: Maximus the Confessor's Hopeful Pedagogy," by Hans Boersma. As long as communication has existed in written forms, reading has demanded one must master technical abilities prescribed by any language. Mastering those technical abilities, however, is only the beginning of what is demanded by the practice of reading. Such a practice routinely requires individuals to ask themselves to what end they are seeking to engage the thoughts of others and, in turn, what virtues may be needed as well as what vices may need to be avoided. This side of eternity, we may never be able to know in full what the author of any particular text intended to communicate. Reading, however, is the hopeful educational practice that teaches us such an effort is worthwhile. As a theologian and clergyperson, Hans Boersma invested a significant portion of his career coming to terms with how reading to a proper end allows one to appreciate how God and beings created in God's image communicate with one another. He offers insights from that work drawn from his experience in parish settings as well as more formal educational settings.

Chapter six is "Prophets and Poets at the Apocalypse: Writing as a Hopeful Educational Practice," by Jessica Hooten Wilson. As with reading, writing also demands one must master technical abilities prescribed by any language. Some individuals even imagine ways those abilities are able to approach what others deem as art. Most writing, while perhaps not art, still reflects the qualities of a hopeful educational practice in that it embodies the belief that one has something worthwhile to share. That which is worthwhile may not immediately prove edifying. By its very definition, hope may first drive people to confront hard realities so that some reflection of the promise of the created order may eventually come to fruition. As a professor leads students through the great texts, Jessica Hooten Wilson explores that promise in the writing of others while also practicing it in her own critically acclaimed writing.

She thus draws on those lessons as a means of inspiring others to reflect upon what writing offers.

Chapter seven is "'Arduous and Difficult to Obtain': Teaching as a Hopeful Educational Practice," by David I. Smith. Due to the significant role individuals who accept the calling to the academic vocation play, Scripture includes warnings to individuals who exercise that calling poorly. Teachers understandably need to possess a certain competence in relation to the materials they share. Those warnings, however, arguably have even more to do with why one teaches than what one teaches. Long after students forget the details of a particular topic offered on any given day, the manner in which the practice of teaching informed them about what it means to be human, what God may have called them to do with their lives, and to what end are they to exercise those callings will linger. Information matters. As access to information has increased, however, how one is formed to use information is proving more crucial. As an award-winning teacher and one of the leading experts in the practice of teaching, David Smith offers insights from his research and writing as well as the transformative impact of what occurs in the classroom that he has witnessed over the course of his career.

INTENDED AUDIENCE

The audience this volume is designed to serve includes members of at least three different groups. First, we believe individuals who accept the calling to the Christian academic vocation will find these chapters and the insights they offer to be beneficial. Although all the contributors to this volume serve or most regularly interact with collegiate audiences, the insights they offer will also be of value to educators serving in secondary educational settings. As a result, we are hopeful this book will be read by educators on their own as well as educators working together in reading groups.

Second, we believe this book will prove to be of interest to administrators, board members, and denominational officials who regularly interact with church-related educational institutions. These individuals bear the greatest responsibility for charting and implementing the missions of their respective institutions. Many, if not all, of them have found themselves facing the temptations offered by the fearful nature of the culture that emerged in the 2010s. We thus believe this volume and the manner the contributors lend their expertise to unpacking the theological significance of core educational practices will offer encouragement as well as practical guidance concerning how these individuals steward the missions of their respective institutions.

Third, we believe the ways the contributors unpack the theological significance of these core educational practices will prove beneficial to practical theologians and in the courses they lead. As reflected in the growth of related literature, practices such as reading, writing, and teaching, for example, are meeting a need of individuals to think theologically about some of the most basic details of their lives. Several of the contributors to this volume are among the most widely respected authors of that literature. We thus believe this book will prove useful in courses in which faculty members are seeking to introduce their students to such forms of theological thought and, in turn, practice.

Although we believe these chapters and the wisdom found within them offer a sense of encouragement to weary educators, we also believe the way that encouragement comes is via a renewed sense of purpose in one's calling to the Christian academic vocation. Hope was born out of the blood-soaked soil on Calvary into which the cross on which Christ was crucified was staked. From that ground emerges the ability to know that no form of oppression claims the final word. Educators are entrusted with the responsibility of pointing lives to and beyond the cross. Hope emerges when such a vertical horizon comes into focus. As a result, the educational practices detailed in these pages offer an expectation of the world to come that only hope can afford and, by God's grace, to which the Christian educator can bear witness.

ONE

THE CROSS OUR HOPE

The Hope of Education

KEVIN G. GROVE, CSC

THE CHALLENGE OF NAMING THE HOPE of education is not to settle for a hope that is too small or proximate, however worthy such desired hopes might be. The hopes of a degree, a career, great research, or even more humane and just societies are resplendent hopes in themselves that education does and should serve. These hopes are proximate compared with the great hope—life eternal with God.[1]

This chapter suggests that for education, the Christian habit of hope gives fundamental depth to the basic human desire for transcendence. Christian education's preoccupation with a "great hope"—for life eternal that we might share—is not an afterthought, but a teleological grounding that can give life and light to the classroom, the laboratory, and the institutional mission. And this is the challenge for the Christian research university in our time: to articulate and abide a vision of Christian hope

---

[1] I borrow the language of "great hope" from Pope Benedict XVI, who wrote in his encyclical *Spes Salvi* (In Hope We Are Saved): "We need the greater and lesser hopes that keep us going day by day. But these are not enough without the great hope, which must surpass everything else. This great hope can only be God, who encompasses the whole of reality and who can bestow upon us what we by ourselves cannot attain." Pope Benedict XVI, *Spes Salvi*, 2007, §31, at www.vatican .va/content/benedict-xvi/en/encyclicals/documents/hf_ben-xvi_enc_20071130_spe-salvi.html.

true to the Gospels that does not close down inquiry, but enlivens it among all of the diverse participants in an institution's mission.

The theological tradition of practicing hope as a virtue—along with faith and love—points the direction to such a great hope. As a "virtue," hope is constitutionally a practice—a way of journeying through this pilgrim land not as our end, but trusting that God ordained us creatures for more than the broken world of which we know ourselves to be a part. Theologian Dominic Doyle thus defines hope in this way: "Hope is the providential movement toward the future, difficult, yet possible goal of eternal life with God, a journey already 'pioneered' by Christ."[2]

As the movement to eternal life, Christian hope is never separated from its corresponding virtues of faith and love. For hope takes up what faith believes and, as Doyle suggests, "carries it through difficulty unto a deeper, transformed love."[3] And so, hope simultaneously catalyzes closeness with God and a more human world.[4] In what follows, this chapter offers that such a Christian virtue of hope is precisely the habit or practice that might transform the difficult work of education into the concomitant increase of love of God and neighbor.

This chapter proceeds in three parts. The first uses the Christian image of the anchor to bridge the theological hope of the New Testament to our own time, noting the importance of hope for the persecuted along the way. Second, I speak about how this hope in the passion, death, and resurrection of Christ translates into the work of education. To this end, I rely on my own religious community, the Congregation of Holy Cross, a relatively new Catholic religious order founded for the work of education and with the specific charism, or spiritual gift, to connect education and hope. I draw inspiration from Holy Cross founder, Basil Moreau, to demonstrate the connection between hope in Christ and Christian education. The third and final section draws the insights of the first two into habits of hope for education, relying on my own experience

---

[2]Doyle is drawing on Hebrews 12:2. Dominic F. Doyle, *The Promise of Christian Humanism: Thomas Aquinas on Hope* (New York: Herder & Herder, 2012), 95.
[3]Doyle, *Promise of Christian Humanism*, 145.
[4]Doyle, *Promise of Christian Humanism*, 145.

as a faculty member in theology at the University of Notre Dame and the legendary leader of my own institution, Fr. Theodore Hesburgh, CSC. The essay concludes that the virtue of Christian hope is foundational to education—the daily labor through which the growing desire for the great hope of life in Christ might be known, loved, and served in human community.

THE ANCHOR: AN IMAGE OF CHRISTIAN HOPE EVER-ANCIENT, EVER-NEW

From the time of the writing of the New Testament through the present day, hope has figurative expression in the anchor. Appreciating the ever-ancient, ever-new way this single symbol contains a theology of hope establishes the foundation from which the hope of education can be broadly conceived. The symbol of the Christian anchor marked major inflection points in Christian history to rekindle the sort of hope that is transformative of persons and societies.

Hope, in the scriptural witness, is for eternal life. In the letter to the Hebrews, the author writes of the unchangeable reality of God's promise: "We have this hope, a sure and steadfast anchor of the soul, a hope that enters the inner shrine behind the curtain, where Jesus, a forerunner on our behalf, has entered, having become a high priest forever according to the order of Melchizedek" (Heb 6:19-20, NRSVUE).[5] The key movement yielding hope is the entry into the inner shrine—the holy of holies. Christ is not only claimed as a new high (and eternal) priest, but also as one who is mediating life to human persons out of his own passion, death, and resurrection. Thus the hope to which the anchor points is life and light. We creatures, for our part, cannot create or produce such a hope. However, we might participate in it once it is delivered by Christ.

Since Christ's passion, death, and resurrection have offered this hope in full, the cross becomes a source of hope. The anchor symbolically captures both parts of this reality: the crossbar of christological promise

---

[5] All scriptural citations are from the NRSVUE unless otherwise noted.

as well as the mooring of the crown's (the bottom of an anchor's) stability in having been once and ever given. The renowned patristic preacher in the Greek east, John Chrysostom, claimed for his congregation that the anchor is the icon of the hope of Christ: when dropped from a vessel into the sea, the anchor of Christ does not allow even ten thousand winds to agitate it or move it around.[6]

This theology visually animated the lives of Christians in the earliest centuries. If one visits today the catacombs of the early Christian martyrs from Roman persecutions, one will find imagery that all has to do with the hope of resurrection to new life.[7] These ancient tomb coverings, as well as the paintings inside of them, feature anchors as a dominant symbol. In the places both where Christians were buried and early martyrs lost their lives in times of persecution, the anchor claims both their lives and their deaths as testimonies to a singular hope.

By the sixth century, Fortunatus famously wrote the hymn still used in worship today that expresses the Passion of Christ as the great hope: *O Crux ave, spes unia* ("O hail the cross, our only hope").[8] Frequently enough, this verse appears iconographically with anchors. With arms out like a cross, the anchor recalls the passion, death, and resurrection of Christ while making a nod to the current condition of the living in its mooring effect.

As I suggested at the outset, the anchor is a symbol of hope both ever-ancient and ever-new. I live and work at the University of Notre Dame, a Catholic university of the Congregation of Holy Cross, the religious order of which I am part. Notre Dame is the best known of a worldwide network of Holy Cross schools and provides a great number of culturally intelligible religious images, from the *Word of Life* mural in granite on

---

[6]John Chrysostom, "Homily 11 on the Letter to the Hebrews" in *Nicene and Post-Nicene Fathers,* vol. 14 (New York: Christian Literature Company, 1889), 418-22.

[7]Jason Whitlark shows the connections between catacomb anchors and the letter to the Hebrews in "Funerary Anchors of Hope and Hebrews: A Reappraisal of the Origins of the Anchor Iconography in the Catacombs of Rome," *Perspectives in Religious Studies* 48, no. 3: 219-41. Other instances of resurrection imagery in the catacombs include the prophet Jonah (referenced by Christ and emergent from three days in the fish).

[8]Fortunatus's hymn, *Vexilla Regis Prodeunt,* was originally used for Good Friday in Christian liturgy and is still used in Catholic, Anglican, and Lutheran worship during Passiontide.

the Hesburgh Library (known affectionately as "Touchdown Jesus" to football fans) to the statue of Mary the Mother of God on the golden dome of the Main Building on campus as a model of one who learns truths human and divine. ("Mary treasured all these words and pondered them in her heart" [Lk 2:19]).

What most visitors to the university miss, however, is that these icons of Catholic higher education are undergirded by a more subtle symbolic register: the anchor. For example, beneath the golden dome of the Main Building, on the center of the mosaic floor, is a cross flanked by anchors with the words *spes* and *unica*, meaning "hope" and "only," underneath. The cross flanked by anchors is found on the cornerstones of buildings, in entryways, on seals, signs, doorposts, and even in the marching band's formation on the football field antecedent to games. Holy Cross priests and brothers of campus wear the same symbol around their necks as a sign of their religious profession. These multivalent markers offer a visual claim that the ancient image of the great Christian hope—the anchor—has even now a claim to make on the daily work of a modern research university. To understand how it does means looking briefly to Basil Moreau, the founder of Holy Cross, and his vision for education and Christian hope.

From Anchor in Christ to Christian Education: The Hope of Education

As a religious order in the Catholic Church, the Congregation of Holy Cross is much younger than the ancient Greek monasteries or the Benedictine tradition. Formed in the nineteenth century, the Congregation of Holy Cross emerged from a societal rupture in France that brought the need for hope. Basil Moreau, a French priest and ultimately the founder of Holy Cross, saw as a child the devastation wrought by the French Revolution; as an adult he answered the call for societal and ecclesial renewal through education. In short, the experience of the desolation of the French Revolution and its aftermath—sometimes literally passion and death—also served as sites for hope of resurrection. Three parts of this story are important for this chapter: the desolation of the

French Revolution; education as a work configured to the hope of Christ; that educators' work might be witnessing to that great hope.

Overstating the challenges that the French Revolution ushered in for individuals who lived in its wake in the countryside of France proves difficult. It overhauled society at every level—and it overhauled every level of the Catholic Church in France as well. For Basil Moreau, growing up outside of the city of Le Mans, the effects of the revolution were felt most pointedly in the decimation of education. Religious priests, brothers, and sisters were either killed or exiled during the revolution or its aftermath; the terror ended the work they provided in parishes and schools. In France, a 70 percent drop in the number of students attending university occurred, along with a 7 percent drop in the national literacy rate.[9]

Moreau himself came of age as an educator in this postrevolutionary era. As a young priest, he taught philosophy and later theology at a diocesan seminary, distinguishing himself as keenly aware that the postrevolutionary landscape was different from that which had preceded it. He required seminarians to take a course in physics and to read Bacon and Cicero as well as their required courses. He stated he did not wish for students to be ignorant of anything they should know.[10] His vision of education was not simply to go back to what had been before the revolution, but rather to incorporate what he deemed an appropriate dialogue of the tradition of faith with the discoveries of his time.

When Moreau then began the Congregation of Holy Cross in 1837, he merged a group of teaching brothers and a handful of priests and dedicated their efforts to being "educators in the faith," broadly conceived. This humble effort expanded geographically within the first few years. The mission at the University of Notre Dame was up and running already in 1842. Other early missions included sites in New Orleans and what is now Bangladesh, where the order still serves today. That Moreau might have started an order focused on education is hardly new. But context is

---

[9]For more detail on Moreau and this context, see the introduction to Basil Moreau, *Basil Moreau: Essential Writings* (Notre Dame, IN: Ave Maria, 2014), 2-7.

[10]Moreau, "Circular Letter 36," in *Essential Writings*, 416-17.

important. Moreau's mission in education emerged out of a time of darkness—literally when religious educators faced exile or death. That memory, augmented by the work of a worldwide mission, helped Moreau to articulate for his religious priests, brothers, and sisters the understanding of education as connected to the hope of Christ.

Moreau's writings explicitly link Christian hope to Jesus Christ, especially for those priests, brothers, and sisters in his religious family. In his sermons and spiritual exercises, he offers that, having assimilated the thoughts, dispositions, and life of Christ so closely to one's own, the purpose of a Christian is to become—in the words of Saint Paul—another Christ (Gal 2:20). Any priest, brother, or sister who might take up the work of education was to commit to this ongoing conversion to the life of Christ "as the foundation of all your hope."[11]

Education then became the mode of inducting others into the life of hope, a movement from darkness to light or death to life. Moreau is the first person I can identify in the theological tradition who refers to education as a "work of the resurrection."[12] It is a remarkable contention. For by it, Moreau does not mean only the study of Scriptures and the tradition of the Christian life—though those are certainly foundational. Rather, he sees in the entire process of an education the growth in virtue whereby one learns through a paschal process.

When I explain this connection to my own students, I often ask them to think of something they have learned in college that they will never forget. This request rules out the sort of "knowledge" that one learns temporarily by cramming for a test or superficially by skimming. But real knowledge, the sort that is lasting and has an impact on one's life and choices, often emerges from the challenge of learning that can be put in paschal terms—in short, the carrying of a cross.

Perhaps on the way to real learning one might fall or fail not only once but two or three times. Perhaps on the way to real learning, one might need someone else to carry one's burden for a time. Others might assist

---

[11]See, for a representative example, Moreau, "Sermon on the Reception of the Habit for Carmelite Sisters," in *Essential Writings,* 199.

[12]Moreau, "Christian Education," in *Essential Writings*, 376.

by wiping one's face or standing alongside in endurance, love, and friendship during the darkest or most challenging of times. In short, real learning might spiritually require the sort of losing one's life in order to find it that Christ promises as the condition of discipleship. Yet the experience of having acquired learning that will last rises up within the self like new life. Learning, in some small but nevertheless analogous way, is an experience of resurrection.

So for Moreau, the work of learning in every discipline that a student should know—from the sciences through the arts and technical studies—is an arena for the cultivation of just such a hope. For the hope of acquisition of knowledge, understanding, wisdom, and truth does not circumvent but, rather, hints at the very cross and resurrection paradigm. School studies might teach one to rise again. They can enkindle desire and appreciation for the great hope of Christian life.

A qualification must be made at this point. Anyone who has studied the classics knows the phrase *pathei-mathos* in ancient Greece was connected to the idea that learning emerged from suffering and suffering correlatively from learning. From Aeschylus's *Agamemnon* to the writings of Aristotle, wisdom might emerge from and even require suffering at various points. What Moreau offers is not merely the Greek formulation baptized, but rather a different teleological orientation entirely.

The Christian hope of education is not merely that one would gain knowledge or skill, though both of those are the products of education. Rather, the Christian hope of education is eternal life in Christ, and a work of resurrection can have its ground of possibility and its consummation in only him. So for Basil Moreau, the hope of education in a decidedly christological key could give a surer, longer, greater hope: eternal life. But simultaneously, Moreau rooted the search for that eternal hope in the learning that befits each discipline and its appropriate modes of discovery.

For Moreau, the hope that is imaged by the anchor of the cross becomes the model for Christian education. The hope of Christ's death and resurrection supplied the hope of learning in mathematics, physics, history, and business with new potentiality for human virtue and goodness. This understanding was not limited to the person as an individual, but for the entirety of the Christian community.

At the end of his "Christian Education," after Moreau described the vocation of Christian educators as taking up the work of the resurrection, he goes on to describe its communal effect. By this work, his hearers are to "prepare the world for better times than our own."[13] For each student is part of not only a family now, but also perhaps the foundation of a future one. And so, the image of hope is never a singular endeavor but one in which the virtue grows in those who know its struggle. They pass from the isolation of ignorance over into communion of truth with each other. In this way, hope's promise is never the isolation of the individual who suffers alone, but rather the communal telos of life and light in Christ. Those who practice hope in the work of learning are those who can know and inhabit in some small way the union that will be complete only at Christ's return.

Basil Moreau helped to connect for us the image of the anchor not as a static hope but as the transformative great hope in Christ that can enliven the work of education. He responded to a world in need not simply by beginning schools and providing content, but also by seeing that the work of education was potentially a unique modality in which to teach Christian hope. Inasmuch as he saw in education a work of resurrection, he seeded the entire process of learning and teaching with the potential to practice the virtue of hope.

For the individual learner and teacher alike, the processes of learning and teaching take on a paschal character—learning to die and rise in a daily manner that capacitates one more fully as an individual to appreciate and prepare for resurrection in Christ. At the same time, this individual learning has a communal and human effect.[14] It means that teachers and learners alike learn to accompany one another in suffering and in cultivating hope. It bonds persons together in communion that promises a different society—one of life and light.

---

[13]Moreau, "Christian Education," in *Essential Writings*, 376.
[14]Benedict XVI uses a similar logic in *Spes Salvi* (§§ 35-48): Our hope is measured by our action and by our care for those who are suffering.

As such, the anchor of hope, when a paradigm for a university, is a "big idea" that changes the shape of research and teaching. I offer to my students when I teach them about Christ's resurrection that such an event has ramifications throughout history and is the raison d'etre for their being in my classroom in the 2020s. It is always remarkable to see their faces when I make this claim regarding their work and struggle.

HABITS OF HOPE: A CASE STUDY AND SIGNPOSTS FOR THE TASK AHEAD

The question remains of how it is that the great hope—of eternal life in Christ—might inform the smaller hopes in which universities so frequently take stock: progress, discovery, teaching, and learning.

I wish to offer a concrete example from my own Department of Theology at the University of Notre Dame. Faced with the challenge of articulating the coherence of a Catholic liberal arts core curriculum to our students, we faculty members have found that students all too often perceive core requirements as boxes to check or courses that might require "getting through" en route to a degree or career trajectory. The effect of this sort of thinking is not the integration of education but rather a fragmentation and compartmentalization that prioritizes usefulness toward a career trajectory or other goal.

As a counterpoint, our department set out to write a single paragraph that could be placed at the top of our syllabi, explaining what the core curriculum does. This could then be followed by our own brief course description, claiming how our course contributes to this mission. So, for instance, when I teach our introductory Foundations of Theology course, I put this core paragraph at the top of my syllabus followed by a second paragraph of how the objectives of my course flow from and contribute to this vision. I take time on the first day of class to explain both to my students.

I will produce the paragraph in full here and then below speak about its movements. The two sources that it draws from are Notre Dame's Mission Statement as well as a key global document in twentieth-century

Catholic thought on higher education, *Ex Corde Ecclesiae* by John Paul II.[15]

> The Catholic intellectual tradition affirms that the desire and capacity for truth and justice are gifts of God, which are given for the sake of the full flourishing of the human person and the building up of the common good. Guided by this hope, Notre Dame is dedicated to "the pursuit of truth for its own sake" (*ND Mission Statement*), from which springs that *gaudium de veritate*, "the joy of searching for, discovering, and communicating truth in every field of knowledge" (*Ex corde ecclesiae* §1). The University is a community of students and faculty of various faiths, backgrounds, and gifts, laboring in the common pursuit of wisdom. Together we seek through the core curriculum "an intelligibility and a coherence to all reality" (*NDMS*), moving from truths as discovered and taught by individual disciplines toward the ultimate unity of truth. Rather than an arbitrary set of requirements, the core curriculum is a doorway inviting us to consider a final integration: a "higher synthesis" (*Ex corde ecclesiae* §16) of science and wisdom, faith and reason, theory and practice, indeed, of all things created and uncreated in Christ, "in whom all things hold together" (Col. 1:17).

The paragraph, composed in 2018, is only five sentences, but taken together they make a claim concerning how we as faculty members of a university might invite students into our mission, which may not be self-evident to them (i.e., that core requirements have an integrative nature), and make a claim on a greater hope. The first sentence offers in a single line the Christian hope, placing in relation the person, the community, and God. God capacitates humans to desire truth and justice. These are gifts of our human condition that, when fostered, draw us into full flourishing in ourselves and closer with one another. That is the great hope that guides the claims of sentences two (the university in pursuit of truth), three (the collaborative nature of the pursuit of truth), and four and five (the higher synthesis to which a core curriculum as induction into the truth leads).

---

[15]For the Notre Dame Mission Statement, see www.nd.edu/about/mission/; for John Paul II's *Ex Corde Ecclesiae*, see www.vatican.va/content/john-paul-ii/en/apost_constitutions/documents /hf_jp-ii_apc_15081990_ex-corde-ecclesiae.html.

When I read this paragraph to my students on the first day of their freshman year, I suggest it should reframe the way they go about their core requirements, including my own course. Their requirement in mathematics is not simply about the acquisition of calculus, but about becoming capacitated for the truth in the unique mode that mathematics provides. The same might be said of their study of foundations of theology, which is the discipline that deals with divine revelation as a subject of inquiry on its own terms and logic.

I am aware enough that all humans from time to time work to "get through it." But hope as a virtue or habit means that those who labor through core requirements and assignments might do so with the goal that a higher synthesis and purpose is possible. And, for the Catholic core curriculum as my colleagues and I have articulated it, this configuration to the truth is possible on account of Christ who in himself made truth incarnate—and lifted the study of truth in all forms and disciplinary disclosures.

This paragraph concerning a core curriculum is in many ways a small and humble example, but it enacts the logic inherent in practicing as a virtue the "great hope" of Christian education. The paragraph makes a claim on the virtue of hope that is to guide the truth-seeking of the university, the contribution of its diverse students, faculty, and staff, and finally the hope for synthesis that is uniquely made possible in Christ. The paragraph is a witness both to student and professor alike that the lecture hall is not merely a place of transaction—performance for grade, or information exchange—it is an arena to grow the capacity and desire for truth that makes us more human and interconnected. Virtue cannot be legislated, but such witness sets forth the bold claim that in each class session it is possible.

The profound humility that comes from this sort of hope requires that the task ahead hardly be a triumphal one. Rather, the practice or habit of hope is one that recapitulates the paschal structure and challenge of coming to be true. For the Christian university that speaks uniquely of the hope that its mission witnesses, the regular functions of universities need more than ephemeral connections to the great hope of their calling. The

Christian university that thrives in the future will be one in which a vision of fundamental research across the disciplines can be inspired by the great hope rather than by seeing its christological root as a sign of contradiction. The Christian university that thrives in the future will be one in which the truths that we study are both self-implicating and constitutive of human communion. And the Christian university's practice of hope—as emergent from the passion, death, and resurrection of Christ—will be measurable by the extent to which it finds and embraces those places in the human community most afflicted by pain and suffering. Communal, eternal, practiced as daily habit, and anchored in Christ, Christian education will be known either by the greatness or the paucity of its hope.

The Enduring Legacy of Theodore M. Hesburgh, CSC

In 1962, the University of Notre Dame's president, Fr. Theodore Hesburgh, CSC, was interviewed for the cover story of *TIME* concerning the nature of Catholic education.[16] Honest about the seeming challenge of a Catholic university, the article opens by quoting George Bernard Shaw, who famously claimed a Catholic university was a contradiction in terms. Shaw's claim, of course, has hardly faded, still construed as an opposition between faith and reason, theology and science, the work of a church and a university. But it is worth considering these false oppositions as limitations on hope.

What if faith, theology, and the work of churches was not somehow a limit on what the human might do, but the call to a greater hope of our integrated search for truth, beauty, and goodness? Hesburgh, in the article, makes a unique claim in response to the logic of Shaw, offering, "We are men committed to Truth, living in a world where most academic endeavor concerns only natural truth, as much separated from supernatural truth, the divine wisdom of theology, as sinful man was separated from God before the Incarnation."

Hesburgh understands the Catholic university as doing a work of mediation: "We must somehow match secular or state universities in their

---

[16]*TIME*, "Education: God and Man at Notre Dame," February 9, 1962, at https://content.time.com /time/subscriber/printout/0,8816,938327,00.html.

comprehension of a vast spectrum of natural truths in the arts and sciences, while at the same time we must be in full possession of our own true heritage of theological wisdom."[17] For Hesburgh, this was a commitment to "total truth"—not only those truths discoverable by our own production in the natural order but also those revealed. The unique voice of the Christian university is that all these truths are on the table, where at other places those truths of revelation would be out of bounds.

Hesburgh's hope was for a "possible renaissance" and this claim was depicted visually on the cover of the same *TIME* issue. The cover of the magazine is a painting of Hesburgh holding open a book with two distinct features. The pages of the book, open to the viewer, have on one page an image of Giotto di Bondone's *Madonna Enthroned* from the Uffizi Gallery in Florence. The second and third pages of the book have scientific and mathematical texts. There is more to this pairing than the simple putting together of a Marian image suggestive of Notre Dame with some aspect of reason or research. The Giotto *Madonna* is from an altarpiece that is largely considered to be one of the earliest works of the Florentine Renaissance. That Renaissance gave humanity Brunelleschi's architectural dome, Michelangelo's masterpieces, and other instances of the theologically inspired flourishing of the arts and sciences. Hesburgh's claim, and the reason for the *Madonna* as he is holding it, is that the Catholic university is a possible site of a new renaissance—one in which inquiry into "total" truth—natural and revealed—might be so energizing as to inspire the full flourishing of the human person and the common good.

I reside in a residence hall at Notre Dame with 221 students. A couple of years ago, I was given a reproduction of Giotto's *Madonna* from a friend. I hung Giotto's *Madonna* in the small reading nook in my hallway and framed the cover of *TIME* on which Hesburgh was the feature, hanging it alongside the Giotto reproduction. For each class of students who move into my dorm, I explain the significance of the claim that the painting makes on their four years in the hall—that they are themselves, if they are up for it, part of a new renaissance.

---

[17]*TIME*, "Education: God and Man."

Day in and day out, many parts of life happen in the chairs of that nook right outside my door. Families are called, friends gather, romances begin and even end, homework is done, and papers are written into the wee hours of the morning. But this ordinary space for college life is marked by a structural claim of a higher purpose. And my hope is that, when my neighbors consider their time in what they affectionately have termed "the renaissance lounge," the very claim on the higher purpose will have helped them to foster in themselves the habit of our great hope.

Ultimately, the hope of Christian education is one that lets the promise of life in Christ inspire the flourishing of all other hopes. Engaging faith and incarnate in love, Christian hope is not notional but an anchor—the gritty, enduring, communion-making work by which the teaching, research, and communal life of the university are ennobled to their fullest. In the pursuit of truth, we might become true not alone but together. Thus, the hope of education, given by Christ, is not the limit on truth, but the daily demand for its fullness.

TWO

PAST, PRESENT, AND FUTURE

Integration as a Hopeful
Educational Practice

PHILIP GRAHAM RYKEN

MANY OF THE STRONGEST ADVOCATES for the integration of faith and learning lived in troubled times, when hope was hard to sustain, and many critics doubted the value or long-term efficacy of Christ-centered higher education.[1] Their perseverance and the enduring contributions they made to Christian intellectual history can inspire our own faithful practice of faith integration in the face of all present and future challenges.

HARD TIMES FOR CHRISTIAN HIGHER EDUCATION

Consider Cassiodorus. An eyewitness to social unrest, military conflict, and imperial collapse, Roman senator Magnus Aurelius Cassiodorus left his high public office around AD 540 and returned to his native Squillace

---

[1]Thoughtful input from friends who serve as presidents of schools that advance the cause of faith and learning improved this essay: Robin Baker (George Fox University), Gayle Beebe (Westmont College), Michael Lindsay (Taylor University), Kim Phipps (Messiah University), and Deana Porterfield (Seattle Pacific University). All information about faith integration on their campuses comes from these colleagues. Generous insights from colleagues at Wheaton College also strengthened my work: Sarah Borden, Jeffry Davis, Richard Gibson, Timothy Larsen, Karen Anhwei Lee, and Gregory Morrison.

to build up what he called the *Vivarium*—a life-giving monastic community for faith and learning.[2]

The Bible was squarely at the center of Cassiodorus's educational vision. The Vivarium was a place for the daily recitation and memorization of sacred Scripture. Yet the Vivarium was also a place for serious scholarship in other ways than biblical studies, complete as it was with a classical library and a scriptorium for copying learned manuscripts. The erstwhile senator's two-volume magnum opus—*The Sacred and Divine Institutes*—covered geography, astronomy, logic, rhetoric, mathematics, and history as well as theology and biblical studies. Essentially, *The Institutes* was a tour de force in the integration of faith and learning.

Cassiodorus self-consciously stood in a venerable intellectual tradition: Cicero, Quintilian, Aristotle. Rather than advancing his own insights, he wanted to commend "the words of the ancients, which are rightly praised and gloriously proclaimed to future generations." But Cassiodorus wanted to do more than preserve the learning of the past; he also wanted to promote a thriving Christian intellectual culture. "When I became aware of the fervent desire for secular learning," he wrote, "through which a great multitude hope to obtain worldly wisdom, I was deeply grieved, I confess, for while secular authors without a doubt have a powerful and widespread tradition, the Holy Scripture wanted for public teachers." Cassiodorus thus lamented the lack of public Christian witness, which he believed could be strengthened by integrating faith and learning under the lordship of Jesus Christ.

Writing more than a millennium later, the Puritan John Milton had similar hopes for Christian education. He composed his seminal essay "Of Education" in 1644, at a time of political polarization, religious turmoil, and sometimes violent unrest. Yet Milton calmly and hopefully argued that a generous and distinctly Christian education had a sacred purpose in secular society. "The end of learning," he wrote, "is to repair the ruin of our first parents by regaining to know GOD aright, and out of

---

[2]The quotations and anecdotes in the following paragraphs are drawn from Richard Hughes Gibson, "The Cassiodorus Necessity: Keeping Faith Alive Through Christian Education," *The Plough Quarterly* (September 2020).

that knowledge to love Him, to imitate Him, to be like Him."[3] In short, education that integrates faith with learning is a form of divine grace for healing a wounded world.

Cassiodorus and Milton held on to the hope of Christian education and advanced its cause in cultural settings hardly conducive to the life of the mind. We could cite many other examples, from Alcuin to Calvin to Dorothy L. Sayers. Like these faithful educators, the seventeenth-century Moravian reformer John Amos Comenius served God in war-ravaged, plague-ridden times. Comenius began his *Pampaedia* ("universal education") by affirming his expansive hope that through Christian education,

> not just one particular person be fully formed into full humanity, or a few, or even many, but every single person, young and old, rich and poor, of high and low birth, men and women, in a word, everyone who is born: so that in the end, in time, proper formation might be restored to the whole human race, throughout every age, class, sex, and nationality.[4]

Life was not much easier in Moravia than it was in Mexico City, where around the same time Sister Juana Ines de la Cruz sometimes sat in her convent worrying that "sheer love of learning" might distract her from the love of God. But Sister Juana, too, began to think that the liberal arts could be brought under the lordship of Jesus Christ. "All things proceed from God," she reasoned, "who is at once the center and the circumference from which all existing lines proceed and at which all end up."[5]

Closer to the present, C. S. Lewis's famous sermon "Learning in War-Time" provided a spirited defense of university education in the context of World War II.[6] Lewis preached in December 1939, not long after England had declared war on Germany. Some were arguing that holding lectures was irresponsible or even impossible, as were writing papers and

---

[3]John Milton, "Of Education," The John Milton Reading Room, at https://milton.host.dartmouth .edu/reading_room/of_education/text.shtml.

[4]John Amos Comenius, *Pampaedia: lateinischer Text und deutsche Ubersetzung*, ed. Dmitrij Tsche- zewsku (Heidelberg: Quelle & Meyer, 1960), I:6, in "Educating Humans: A Comenian Anniver- sary," David I. Smith, *Christian Scholar's Review* (November 15, 2020).

[5]Juana Ines de la Cruz, *A Sor Juana Anthology*, trans. Alan S. Trueblood (Cambridge, MA: Harvard University Press, 1990), 216.

[6]C. S. Lewis, "Learning in War-Time," in *The Weight of Glory and Other Addresses* (New York: Macmillan, 1949).

sitting for exams. Lewis believed otherwise and argued that world war was not a new situation but rather an intensification of the normal human condition, in which life and death always hang in the balance. If we defer higher learning until a time fully congenial to educational pursuits, we might wait forever. The time to pursue a deeper intellectual understanding of God's world and our place in it is always *now*.

By their courage and the quality of their work, these notable Christian thinkers inspire perennial hope for faith and learning. Hard times for Christian higher education are here again in the twenty-first century. The reasons for this are too familiar and too manifold to require much rehearsal. They include the lingering impact of a global pandemic, widespread skepticism about the value of advanced education, shifting and declining demographics, diminished operating margins resulting in program reductions and school closures, culture-wide hostility to core principles of Christian ethics, the brave new world of artificial intelligence, changing legal standards for college admissions, the fragmentation of American evangelicalism, and much more.

If the history of Christian education is any indication, however, these same challenges may afford us the opportunity to do some of our best spiritual and intellectual work. Certainly, this is an ideal time to display the difference it makes to understand the world in Christian perspective and to pursue learning out of love for Jesus Christ and the world he made, including the people he made and is remaking according to his image. Believing that all truth really is God's truth, we seek to cultivate curiosity about creation, a love for great books, an appetite for truth and beauty, a lifelong passion for the life of the mind, the capacity to communicate the gospel across cultures, and the spiritual and intellectual virtues that promote wisdom. If we hold on to hope, our spirited defense and disciplined integration of faith and learning may inspire other thoughtful leaders to take up the high calling of Christian higher education in their generation.

DEFINITION AND DEFENSE

We begin with a foundational question: What is "the integration of faith and learning"?

To define our terms, the word *faith* refers to something more than personal trust in Jesus Christ or the pious practice of Christian discipleship. It refers more expansively to the full content of Christian theology—everything Christians believe on the basis of Scripture, centering on the divine person and redeeming work of Jesus Christ.

The word *learning* refers to everything we can know about the world around us, including about human culture and experience. More specifically, it refers to academic study in humanities and the sciences, including the social sciences, as well as the visual, musical, and performing arts.

The word *integration* indicates that two things need to be brought closer together in a union or synthesis, with the goal of displaying their interconnections. In the context of Christian higher education, faith integration refers to the exploration of academic disciplines with the full resources of Christian conviction. William Hasker briefly describes "faith-learning integration" as "a scholarly project whose goal is to develop integral relationships which exist between the Christian faith and human knowledge, particularly as expressed in the various academic disciplines."[7] The journal *Christian Higher Education* provides a more comprehensive definition as the basis for further scholarly work in the field:

> Academic faith integration is the work carried out by Christian faculty members when they meaningfully bring the scholarship of their discipline or professional practice and the scholarship representing insights and perspectives from Christian faith into dialogue with each other, applying that dialogue and its results to their research, the courses they teach, and their discipline-related products resulting in disciplinary perspectives that are uniquely informed by faith and/or faith perspectives that are uniquely informed by the discipline or profession.[8]

Integrating faith and learning does not simply mean opening a class session with prayer, although doing so is a wise and holy practice—a way of invoking the blessed presence of the Holy Spirit and setting the

---

[7]William Hasker, "Faith-Learning Integration: An Overview," *Christian Scholar's Review* 21, no. 3 (1992): 234, italics original.
[8]Paul Kaak, "Academic Faith Integration: Introduction to a New Section Within *Christian Higher Education*," *Christian Higher Education* 15, no. 4 (2016): 192, italics original.

classroom apart as one form of sacred space. Nor does faith integration refer merely to presenting a devotional thought at the beginning of class that relates broadly to the content of a course. Doing so may also be spiritually and intellectually beneficial. Yet by themselves—and even taking into account their life-changing power—an opening prayer and Bible reading do not provide the richer understanding that comes with more rigorous and complete faith integration in course lectures and discussions.

To illustrate what is possible, consider what the ethicist and theologian Lewis Smedes writes in his memoir about the personal transformation he experienced in his undergraduate writing course at Calvin College. The life change did not come simply through relevant Scripture and prayer, but through the specific content of the course, as presented in its integral connection to the triune God. In his writing class, Smedes was introduced "to a God the likes of whom I had never even heard about." This God, he was amazed to discover,

> liked elegant sentences and was offended by dangling modifiers. Once you believe this, where can you stop? If the Maker of the Universe admired words well put together, think of how he must love sound thought well put together, and if he loved sound thinking, how he must love a Bach concerto and if he loved a Bach concerto think of how he prized any human effort to bring a foretaste, be it ever so small, of his Kingdom of Justice and peace and happiness to the victimized people of the world. In short, I met the Maker of the Universe who loved the world he made and was dedicated to its redemption. I found the joy of the Lord, not at a prayer meeting, but in English Composition 101.[9]

While it is doubtful whether God is "offended by dangling modifiers" (certainly, he loves people who use them), Smedes was right to be inspired by finding God in the particularities of a college classroom. Properly understood, the integration of faith and learning he experienced at Calvin refers to the comprehensive consideration of academic

---

[9]Lewis Smedes, quoted in Philip Yancey, *A Skeptic's Guide to Faith* (Grand Rapids, MI: Zondervan, 2009), 66.

subject matter in the context of God's truth as revealed in creation and the Word of God, both *inscripturated* and *incarnated* in the person of Jesus Christ.

The Protestant Reformers and their theological descendants rightly emphasized that God has two books for us to read: one of "special" revelation (the Bible) and the other of "general" revelation (creation). The English polymath Sir Thomas Browne testified, "There are two books from whence I collect my divinity: besides that written one of God, another of his servant, nature, that universal and public manuscript that lies expansed unto the eyes of all."[10] This multidimensional understanding of revealed truth opens up the entire universe to our intellectual exploration, and to the possibility of understanding everything in its proper connection to God as Creator and Redeemer.

The integration of faith and learning involves recognizing the many places where human learning converges with revealed truth. Christian scholars test intellectual assumptions according to the touchstone of Scripture and in the process deepen their understandings of both the main principles of academic disciplines and the core tenets of Christian theology.[11] Through rigorous critique, the integration of faith and learning can set academic insights on a stronger foundation—one that rests ultimately on the bedrock of revealed truth. Faith integration also specifies the many places where human learning—in both its fallenness and its finitude—violates the norms of biblical ethics, fails to honor the divine image in human beings, or in other ways falls short of the glory of God. Faculty members who think along these lines can give their students "integrative moments" in the classroom—moments when academic pursuits intersect with the life of faith.[12] Simply put, the integration of faith and learning means "thinking Christianly" about everything.

---

[10]Thomas Browne, *Religio Medici*, I.16, cited at www.encyclopedia.com/education/encyclopedias-almanacs-transcripts-and-maps/two-books; accessed August 8, 2023.

[11]One good place to start learning the history of distinctively Christian approaches to specific academic disciplines is with the useful student guides that David S. Dockery has edited for Crossway Books under the series title Reclaiming the Christian Intellectual Tradition.

[12]Terry Anne Lawrence, Larry D. Burton, and Constance C. Nwosu, "Refocusing on the Learning in 'Integration of Faith and Learning,'" *Journal of Research on Christian Education* 14, no. 1 (Spring 2005): 17-51.

In *The Idea of a Christian College*, philosopher Arthur Holmes offers a definition of faith integration that carries wide influence across Christ-centered higher education. The distinctive contribution of a Christian college, Holmes writes,

> should be an education that cultivates the creative and active integration of faith and learning, of faith and culture . . . it must under no circumstance become a disjunction between piety and scholarship, faith and reason, religion and science. . . . Integration also transcends awkward conjunctions of faith and learning in some unholy alliance rather than a future union. What we need is not Christians who are also scholars but Christian scholars, not Christianity alongside education but Christian education. It shuns tacked-on moralizing and applications. . . . It requires a thorough analysis of methods and materials and concepts and theoretical structures, a lively and rigorous interpretation of liberal learning with the content and commitment of Christian faith.[13]

Of course, these simple definitions need further clarification and amplification.[14] Thinking Christianly needs to be embodied in whole persons who love Christianly and live Christianly.[15] Faith integration also needs to be defended from its detractors. For some philosophers and theologians—such as John Henry Newman, in his seminal book *The Idea of the University*—the liberal arts belong to the earthly order of nature (where even a secular university can cultivate the intellect), not to the heavenly order of grace (which pertains to religion and the church). Theology is a separate branch of knowledge that "does not interfere with the real freedom of any secular science in its own particular department."[16] On this

---

[13]Arthur F. Holmes, *The Idea of a Christian College*, rev. ed. (Grand Rapids, MI: Eerdmans, 1989), 6-7.

[14]For taxonomies of various models for integrating faith and learning, see James Riley Estep Jr., "Faith as the Transformer of Learning: Toward an Evangelical Approach to Faith-Learning Integration in Christian Higher Education," *Christian Education Journal*, 2NS (1998): 59-76, and Ken Badley, "The Faith-Learning Integration Movement in Christian Higher Education: Slogan or Substance?," *Journal of Research on Christian Education* 3, no. 1 (1994): 13-33.

[15]Laurie R. Matthias identifies living examples of embodied integration in "Professors Who Walk Humbly with Their God: Exemplars in the Integration of Faith and Learning at Wheaton College," *Journal of Education and Christian Belief* 12, no. 2 (2008): 145-57. See also Perry L. Glanzer and Nathan F. Alleman, *The Outrageous Idea of Christian Teaching* (New York: Oxford University Press, 2019).

[16]John Henry Newman, *The Idea of the University*, ed. Martin J. Svaglic (Notre Dame, IN: University of Notre Dame Press, 1982), 36 (see also 91-93).

interpretation, the liberal arts and sciences belong to a different domain—one that has value primarily or exclusively for our earthly existence.

However, as we shall see, the argument in this chapter is that human learning is a manifestation of God's common grace that also participates in the everlasting kingdom of God, and that as such it is amenable to integration with faith.

Admittedly, Christian professors are not the only scholars who bring their worldviews into the college classroom. All of us have prior assumptions and intellectual presuppositions that inform and influence what we think and teach. As a result, there is no such thing as totally neutral education. All our studies are influenced to greater or lesser degrees by our spiritual commitments. Inherently and inevitably, the faith of Christian students and faculty members is part of their learning and teaching, whether they are explicit about how this happens or not.

Still, a world of difference exists between unreflective pedagogy and the intentional application of biblical truth and Christian theology to the first principles of academic disciplines across the arts and sciences—what many Christian scholars have come to refer to as "faith integration."

We should acknowledge further that faith and learning were never intended to be separate domains. If trusting in Christ as Savior brings us under his dominion as Lord, then everything in life—including our intellectual pursuits—already belongs to him from the moment we are born again. And if Jesus Christ is Lord of the mind—as he must be if "in him all things hold together" (Col 1:17)—then learning already belongs to our life of faith.[17] Indeed, as Arthur Holmes wrote, "faith affects learning far more deeply than learning affects faith."[18] Yet human beings have a way of bifurcating things that properly belong together, and Christians often put their spiritual experience in a separate category from their education, their entertainment, their daily work, and so on. Hence the need for the integration—or perhaps *re*integration—of learning with faith.

Christian faith proves to be indispensable for a comprehensive understanding of anything; the truths of an academic discipline, in turn, can

---

[17]All Scripture quotations in this chapter are from the ESV.
[18]Holmes, *Christian College*, 46.

serve as a lens to illuminate certain aspects of our faith. Nevertheless, many Christians still have an underlying fear of academic pursuits. Understandable reasons for this include the biblical warning that "'knowledge' puffs up" (1 Cor 8:1). Not many people "should become teachers," advises James the Just, because teachers "will be judged with greater strictness" (Jas 3:1). We can and should acknowledge the dangers of intellectualism. Yet we can do this without abandoning hope in Christian higher education. The life of the mind offers beautiful opportunities as well as subtle temptations. In our lifelong pursuit of learning, we do well to heed the wise moral counsel attributed to Bernard of Clairvaux: "Some seek knowledge for the sake of knowledge; that is curiosity. Others seek knowledge that they may themselves be known; that is vanity. But there are still others who seek knowledge in order to serve and edify others, and that is charity."[19]

In the charitable pursuit of knowledge, we must also take into account what Paul said to the Corinthians about Christian thought and gospel witness. In describing his rigorous engagement with secular culture, the apostle said, "We destroy arguments and every lofty opinion raised against the knowledge of God, and take every thought captive to obey Christ" (2 Cor 10:5). Evidently Paul believed there is moral and intellectual work left for us to do in order to bring faith and learning together. We do not need to refer to this work as "integration." We might refer to it instead as "the captivation of learning by faith." Whatever we call it, the biblical imperative is to surrender our academic work to the lordship of Jesus Christ.

All things considered, "the integration of faith and learning" remains one excellent way to construe the calling of Christian higher education. David S. Guthrie believes, reasonably enough, that the phrase has become a pious shibboleth or an empty cliché—something "used to mean whatever a person or institution wants it to mean."[20] If other terms are more precise or other analogies more apposite, then we should use

---

[19]Bernard of Clairvaux, quoted by Mark R. Schwehn, "The Future of Teaching," in *Rethinking the Future of the University*, ed. David Lyle Jeffrey and Dominic Manganiello (Ottawa, ON: University of Ottawa Press, 1998), 76.

[20]David S. Guthrie, *Dreaming Dreams for Christian Higher Education* (Beaver Falls, PA: Falls City Press, 2020), 20, 22. See also Badley, "Faith-Learning Integration Movement."

them. Wheaton College calls its general education curriculum Christ at
the Core, which is a different way of expressing the centrality of Christ
for academic learning. Mark A. Noll wrote a Christology for academia
titled *Jesus Christ and the Life of the Mind*—another constructive turn of
phrase.[21] Perry Glanzer uses alternative theological nomenclature in ad-
vocating for the *"creation and redemption of scholarship."*[22] Whatever we
label it, our urgent, perennial need is to be intentional about the mind of
Christ informing every aspect of Christian higher education.

RENAISSANCE IN FAITH AND LEARNING

There are many reasons to be hopeful about future prospects for strengthening faith and learning in Christian education worldwide, including the
enduring legacy of Christ-animated learning. Before sharing best practices for faith and learning at Christ-centered colleges and universities,
therefore, a survey of the recent history of faith integration will both
encourage and enlighten. Although the roots of this tradition are as deep
as the ancient Christian communities in Antioch and Alexandria, the
integration of faith and learning flourished even more in the past sev-
enty-five years, when two remarkable thinkers and practitioners proved
to be especially influential in advancing Christian thought by counter-
balancing both secularism and fundamentalism: Carl F. H. Henry and
Frank E. Gaebelein.[23]

Carl Henry is perhaps best known as the leading American evangelical
theologian of the second half of the twentieth century. Henry was instrumental in founding many leading evangelical institutions, including the
National Association of Evangelicals, Fuller Theological Seminary, the
Evangelical Theological Society, and *Christianity Today*. Many of his
books have general relevance for faith integration, including his

---

[21]Mark A. Noll, *Jesus Christ and the Life of the Mind* (Grand Rapids, MI: Eerdmans, 2013).

[22]Perry L. Glanzer, "Why We Should Discard 'the Integration of Faith and Learning': Rearticulat-
ing the Mission of the Christian Scholar," *Journal of Education and Christian Belief* 12, no. 1
(2008): 43, italics original.

[23]Unless otherwise indicated, the brief history that follows is drawn largely from "Architects of
Integration at Wheaton College," part of an invaluable resource collected and curated by Wheaton librarian Gregory Morrison and made available online at https://guides.library.wheaton.edu
/faithandlearning/architects.

manifesto for Christian philosophy, *Remaking the Modern Mind*,[24] and his six-volume magnum opus titled *God, Revelation and Authority*.[25]

But Henry also influenced the course of Christian higher education through seminal articles in the 1950s that began to introduce "integration" as an evangelical vocabulary word. The task of Christian education, he wrote, is "the intellectual integration of life and experience," or "the spiritual and intelligible integration of all life's experience."[26]

Frank Gaebelein's philosophy of Christian education was grounded in his remarkable tenure at Stony Brook School, the college preparatory academy on Long Island (New York) where he served as the founding headmaster for four decades, starting in 1922. Gaebelein's life ambition "was to forge an intellectually credible Christian orthodoxy in the modern world."[27] He advanced this ambition through the students he mentored at Stony Brook and also through two books he published by Oxford University Press in the early 1950s: *Christian Education in a Democracy* (1951) and *The Pattern of God's Truth: Problems of Integration in Christian Education* (1954).

The main "problem" that Gaebelein alluded to in the subtitle of the latter volume was "this matter of integration, or uniting the parts into a living whole," which he further described as "the living union" of a school's "subject matter, administration, and even of its personnel, with the eternal and infinite pattern of God's truth."[28] Integration is no easy task, as Gaebelein knew from leading Stony Brook, but strenuous labor that requires creative problem-solving:

> God's truth is of universal scope. This being the case, every aspect of education must be brought into relation to it. So the problem of integration arises—the word, we are reminded, means "the bringing together of parts into the whole." Our aim will be to point the way to a solution of this

---

[24]Carl F. H. Henry, *Remaking the Modern Mind* (Grand Rapids, MI: Eerdmans 1946).

[25]Carl F. H. Henry, *God, Revelation and Authority* (Waco, TX: Word, 1976-83).

[26]Carl F. H. Henry, "Christian Education and the World of Culture," *Mennonite Quarterly Review* 32, no. 4 (1958): 307, 313.

[27]Cheryl L. Fawcett and Jamie Thompson, "Frank Ely Gaebelein," Biola University, at www.biola .edu/talbot/ce20/database/frank-ely-gaebelein#contributions, accessed January 18, 2024.

[28]Frank E. Gaebelein, *The Pattern of God's Truth: Problems of Integration in Christian Education* (New York: Oxford University Press, 1954), 9-10. See also Frank E. Gaebelein, *Christian Education in a Democracy* (New York: Oxford University Press, 1951).

problem by showing how in some vital particulars Christian education can achieve integration into the all-embracing truth of God.[29]

The influence of these two leading thinkers converged at Wheaton College—where Henry had matriculated in 1939—largely at Gaebelein's insistence. Through their writings, lectures, organizational connections, and personal networks, both Henry and Gaebelein helped to shape intellectual life on campus for decades, especially through their strong personal, influential relationships with the main architects of the faith and learning program that Wheaton started for its faculty in 1969: Hudson T. Armerding and Arthur F. Holmes.

From 1965 to 1982, Hudson Armerding served as Wheaton's fifth president. By his initiative, the college hosted its first faith and learning seminar for new faculty in the summer of 1969. Armerding's strong presidential leadership serves as a reminder that propagating effective faith integration requires more than thought leaders; it also calls for a commitment from a school's chief administrators. "Recognizing that Christian education is unique," Armerding argued, "we must establish our own priorities. There must be the integration of faith with learning and the recognition that a Christian perspective is essential in every aspect of today's life." Wheaton's president believed further that the core text for faith integration was the Bible. "We must bring our knowledge of Scripture to bear on our discipline and on the problems of today's world," he wrote. And we must be "prepared to answer what Scripture tells us about our discipline." The result is *rigorous thought and qualitative work* where academic disciplines are effectively integrated with biblical truth."[30]

As a new initiative, Armerding's project needed outside funding, which ministry-minded Chicago businessman Roy Horsey provided for several years until Wheaton secured a five-year grant from the Lilly Foundation. As with everything else in Christian higher education, the integration of faith and learning requires generous philanthropy—a

---

[29]Gaebelein, *Pattern of God's Truth*, 7-8.
[30]Hudson T. Armerding (1969, 1973), quoted in Morrison, "Architects of Integration."

topic to which we shall return. Making kingdom investments in faith and learning is yet another tangible expression of Christian hope: seeds are sown today in anticipation of tomorrow's harvest.

Naturally enough, President Armerding invited his good friend Frank Gaebelein to lead Wheaton's inaugural faith and learning cohort. Then a new faculty member, Leland Ryken remembers the four-week seminar as wide-ranging and intellectually invigorating, albeit somewhat unsystematic. The sessions were weighted more toward lecture than discussion. Visiting scholars included Clark Pinnock and Calvin Seerveld, lecturing on the doctrine of Scripture and the integration of the arts with Christian faith, respectively.[31]

Wheaton's faith and learning seminar soon became a rite of passage for new faculty members. By 1975, Armerding had transferred its leadership to Arthur Holmes, who also served as chair and professor of philosophy. In following years, the seminar was led by distinguished members of the English Department, Alan Jacobs and Roger Lundin. But for more than a decade, Holmes put his stamp on the seminar, selecting its readings and guiding its dialogues according to the truth of Scripture.

Holmes codified his thinking and popularized faith and learning through his 1975 book *The Idea of the Christian College*, in which the philosopher argued that faith integration fulfills the Bible's first and greatest commandment: "The scholar's love for truth becomes an expression of love for God."[32] Holmes was also compelled by the conviction that "Christian perspectives are all-redeeming and all transforming," which "gives rise to the idea of integrating faith and learning."[33] Stated more succinctly, in a phrase with early Christian roots that often gets repeated around campus, "all truth is God's truth, wherever it be found."[34]

Yet Holmes's approach to faith and learning was neither simplistic nor superficial. "The dream is not of loose conjecture of faith and learning,"

---

[31]Leland Ryken, personal correspondence (August 2023).
[32]Holmes, *Christian College*, 48.
[33]Holmes, *Christian College*, 47.
[34]See Arthur F. Holmes, *All Truth Is God's Truth* (Downers Grove, IL: InterVarsity Press, 1977), 61.

he argued at a Wheaton College retreat, "but of a creative integration, one in which faith guides and inspires understanding and gives meaning to human knowledge and experience, one which is devoted to the lucid articulation of Christian perspectives and their interrelation in a coherent world and life view."[35]

Wheaton's summer faith and learning seminar was only the beginning. *The Idea of the Christian College* was read widely by scholars and administrators in the Christian College Consortium and, later, the Council for Christian Colleges and Universities. Holmes also became a frequent guest speaker on the campuses of other Christ-centered colleges and universities, where he spread the good news of faith integration. Soon other schools developed their own faith and learning programs, modeled after what was happening at Wheaton. This expansion was the tangible fulfillment of the hope that Gaebelein had expressed in a 1971 report to President Armerding: "I am convinced that these Seminars represent a major contribution to the advancement of Christian education on a most critical level. For them to continue and even spread to other colleges might well lead to profound and beneficial effects upon Christian higher education in America."[36]

If anything, Gaebelein's vision was too limited, for the faith integration that made its home at Wheaton College has also become a major focus on Christian campuses in Australia, Canada, Kenya, Indonesia, China, Lithuania, Korea, Uganda, and many other countries. Today Christ-centered colleges and universities around the world—from many different evangelical traditions—seek partnership as they give increased attention to faith integration and develop robust teaching and learning programs for their faculty and students. Intellectual and spiritual formation is not culture-bound, but universally valued by the worldwide church. The storied renaissance of faith and learning in the United States over the past century thus gives us reasonable hope for its continued expansion overseas.

---

[35]Arthur F. Holmes (1967), quoted in Morrison, "Architects of Integration."
[36]Frank Gaebelein, report to President Armerding (August 1971), quoted in Morrison, "Architects of Integration."

BEST PRACTICES FOR FAITH INTEGRATION

Today Wheaton College continues to invest institutional resources to grow its faculty programs for the integration of faith and learning. Some of Wheaton's initiatives—described here alongside examples from other campuses—illustrate some of the many ways healthy programs for faith integration inspire hope for the future of Christ-centered education.

To ensure that faith integration is foundational for new faculty members as they become fully enculturated into the school's intellectual ethos, Wheaton's program begins in a faculty member's first year with the monthly Faith and Teaching Seminar. It continues in earnest during the second year of a tenure-track faculty member's service, with the yearlong weekly seminar in faith and learning first established by Provost Stan Jones in 1997. Currently the Carolyn and Fred McManis Professor of Christian Thought and professor of history, Timothy Larsen leads the program and guides each cohort through readings ranging from Athanasius to J. I. Packer, and from Martin Luther and John Wesley to Anne Bradstreet, Chaim Potok, and Pandita Ramabai. John Henry Newman's *The Idea of a University*—noted previously—is another core text.

The Junior Faculty Seminar in Faith and Learning, as it is called, majors on theology. All questions are welcome—even basic ones. Rather than getting the impression that they need to pretend they know more about evangelical orthodoxy than they really do, seminar participants are warmly invited to acknowledge their theological ignorance so they can truly learn. Nearly all new faculty members earned doctorates at research institutions, where they were schooled in secular perspectives. Such preparation poses a challenge and potentially a risk, as Calvin professor Derek Schuurman explained in an interview with the Council for Christian Colleges and Universities:

> They're basically catechized for seven years in the worldview thinking of their particular discipline, and they get their Ph.D. by being able to articulate the paradigm of their discipline in an acceptable way. Then you bring them into your Christian college, and they really need to be challenged and equipped to question the hidden assumptions in their discipline, the philosophical presuppositions that they've been trained in and

mentored in for six or seven years, and sift them through this comprehensive Christian worldview.[37]

Most new faculty members also lack formal training in Christian doctrine and thus bring limited tools for faith integration to the college classroom—another challenge. Their deep learning in areas of disciplinary expertise needs something to "integrate with," so to speak. Thus, they benefit immensely from spending ninety-five minutes every week in spirited dialogue with fellow learners from a wide spectrum of academic disciplines and evangelical traditions, under the guidance of an experienced theologian.

Note the luxurious time frame: ninety-five minutes—every week—for questions, reflection, and dialogue. Importantly, and indeed necessarily, a substantial endowment provides sufficient funds for each new faculty member to receive a course release to facilitate full participation in the seminar, including the time it takes to do the reading. This generous investment alone is an exercise in hope: hope that gifted young scholars can learn theology across evangelical traditions, incorporate it into their disciplinary thinking, and then make fresh insights on faith and learning accessible to their students.

The next step in Wheaton's required faith and learning program may be the most important: to be eligible for tenure or promotion to the associate rank, each new faculty member must complete a major scholarly paper or artistic or other project integrating faith with learning in his or her academic discipline. Two tenured faculty members serve as readers and conversation partners for each project or paper—typically, a colleague from the same department and someone with expertise in biblical and theological studies.

Writing a first-rate "faith and learning paper" is a communal, multiyear process that culminates in formal approval by the program director and the provost. For many new faculty members, their first serious attempt to put into words what it means to think Christianly about

---

[37]Derek Schuurman, quoted in "A Conversation with Esau McCaulley, Todd Ream, Derek Schuurman, and Andrea Scott," *Advance*, Spring 2023, 23.

their specialization sets a trajectory for their future teaching and perhaps scholarship. Many of these papers are published in *Christian Scholars Review* or discipline-specific journals, such as *Christianity and Literature, Science and Engineering Ethics, Fides et Historia,* and the *Princeton Theological Review.*

Published papers are collected in a permanent digital archive, which librarian Gregory Morrison set up for the benefit of other scholars as part of his own faith and learning project.[38] One paper is honored each year by being selected for The Margaret Diddams Annual Lecture on Faith and Learning, a public event—named in honor of the former provost who initiated the lecture—that elevates the profile of faith integration for students, faculty, and the wider community. Publishing and lecturing are also acts of hope—hope that our words can instruct and inspire other students and scholars across time and space.

A successful faith and learning paper is not meant to be the end but only the beginning of a career-long, ever maturing, lifelong pursuit of scholarship under the lordship of Jesus Christ. To that end, Wheaton offers additional learning opportunities for tenured and nontenured faculty members. Faculty members who teach the First Year Seminar for all new students (more on that below) are required (and paid) to take a weeklong course in the history of evangelical theology, cotaught by two theologians.

Wheaton regularly invites a select cohort of distinguished scholars from other campuses—the Faith and Learning Fellows—to connect with faculty members at special events on campus. Special lectures—which in recent years have featured such notable scholars as Jeremy Begbie, Eleonore Stump, Marilynne Robinson, and Christian Wiman—also grace the campus calendar.

Every year Wheaton College offers an Advanced Faith and Learning seminar, meeting weekly for ninety minutes throughout the school year. Like the Junior Seminar, the Advanced Seminar is multidisciplinary, drawing colleagues from academic departments across campus. To

---

[38]Wheaton College Library, "Integrating Faith and Learning," at https://guides.library.wheaton .edu/faithandlearning.

participate, each faculty member receives a course release and/or honorarium. Senior scholars draft proposals to lead these seminars on topics such as Christianity and the Book; Nationalism; Neuroscience and Personhood; and Virtues, Vices, and Spiritual Disciplines.

These seminars, too, are expressions of hope—hope that Christian scholars can sustain their intellectual curiosity, continue learning Bible and theology, become an ever-better version of themselves, and keep making culture-shaping contributions throughout their academic careers.

Wheaton's general education curriculum—Christ at the Core—puts faith integration to the test. All undergraduates take both a First Year Seminar and an Advanced Integration Seminar—classes of some twenty students that focus on reading, writing, and discussion. In fine liberal arts fashion, topics for the First Year Seminar explore the question "What is the good life?" from various social, philosophical, literary, or scientific vantage points. About two-thirds of the readings are standardized, to afford all new students shared intellectual experiences, but faculty members freely incorporate their own areas of specialization into one-third of the coursework.

Later on, students in the Advanced Integration Seminar—often co-taught to foster interdisciplinary approaches—explore solutions to major world problems. To help ensure they accomplish their full educational purpose, the learning outcomes for both seminars relate explicitly to the integration of faith and learning. This experience provides campus-wide accountability for the vital task of integrating faith with learning in the classroom.

The First Year and Advanced Integration Seminars help to anchor Wheaton's enduring commitment to faith and learning, as does the Senior Capstone, which comes in the final year of a student's pathway through the general education curriculum. Although this seminar is taught within an academic department, the purpose is not to address advanced topics in a chosen discipline but to help students reflect on what they have learned over four years of faith integration in classes across the curriculum. This expense too is an expression of hope—hope that a Christ-centered education proves to be more than the sum of its parts as it becomes integrated into the life calling of a graduate.

To be clear, faith integration is not limited to a handful of lectures and seminars at Wheaton but expected in every class on campus. All course evaluations—whether they are filled out by students or conducted by colleagues—include questions about a faculty member's ability to integrate learning with faith in the classroom. Similarly, all tenure and promotion applications require candidates themselves, their faculty peers, a department chair or program director, an academic dean, and the faculty personnel committee to assess progress in faith integration.

Other Christ-centered campuses developed comparable and, in many cases, exceptional programs for helping faculty members integrate learning with faith in their pedagogy and research. Taylor University's Bedi Center for Teaching and Learning Excellence oversees a Faculty Faith Integration Seminar that is similar to Wheaton's, with perhaps greater emphasis on teaching faculty the literature on faith and learning and thus introducing them to various models for faith integration. In addition to writing the first draft of their "faith-discipline integration paper," the teacher-scholars in Taylor's second-year seminar write a "philosophy of faith-pedagogy" and create "faith-classroom integration" assignments over the course of their seminar.

At Seattle Pacific University, faculty members can strengthen their grasp of Christian doctrine in relation to their academic disciplines by joining the Theological Integration Fellows Program and taking seminary coursework toward a certificate in theology. As at Wheaton, the vital work of faith integration is carried forward through the collaboration of faculty members in the liberal arts and sciences with colleagues in Bible and theology.

In keeping with the stated goal of helping students "explore the relevance and mutual connectedness of the Christian faith and educational pursuits," Messiah University launches first-semester faculty with a Provost's Seminar. The dialogue on faith integration continues through highly valued "Christian Scholarship Colloquies." In keeping with the university's anabaptist heritage, these small group discussions take place over dinner, with second-year scholars engaging in generative conversations on the connections between faith and learning. Messiah typically uses the phrase "Christian faith and academic vocation" to describe its long-term aspirations for the flourishing of its faculty members.

Academic vocation is also an important concept in George Fox University's formal three-year course sequence for faculty development, which covers faith and learning in year one, faith and scholarship in year two, and faith and vocation in year three. In keeping with the school's Quaker heritage, George Fox adds spiritual formation as a critical component of faith integration. By nurturing the life of the Spirit through corporate worship and incorporating spiritual disciplines into faculty development, the university seeks to nurture the spiritual as well as the intellectual life of its community.[39]

In addition to campus-wide programs for faculty development in faith integration, many Christian colleges and universities have programs, centers, lectures, and institutes for integrating faith with learning in specific areas of academic interest. Westmont's Annual Conversation on the Liberal Arts—sponsored by the college's Gaede Institute for the Liberal Arts—is a notable example with national influence.

Other efforts at faith integration are more campus- or region-specific, such as Seattle Pacific's Center for Faithful Business, Wheaton's Center for Faith, Politics, and Economics, Messiah's Central Pennsylvania Forum on Faith and Science, or the Engineering Your Soul program that George Fox runs for teachers and students in its thriving school of engineering—an evening dialogue on assigned reading that finds expression in spiritual disciplines.

As important as formal programs are for developing sound habits of faith integration, what matters as much—or more—is the mindset. The colleges and universities that offer the most hope for the future of Christian higher education maintain high aspirations for academic culture and are suffused with faith integration—what Timothy Larsen

---

[39]For more on George Fox's program for faculty development, see Patrick Allen and Kenneth Badley, *Faith and Learning: A Practical Guide for Faculty* (Abilene, TX: Abilene Christian University Press, 2014).

aptly describes as "an institutional integrative ethos."[40] When this mindset is firmly in place, it naturally will find expression in ways that are consistent with the distinctive mission and tradition of each institution.

THE RESURRECTION AND ASCENSION OF FAITH AND LEARNING

This chapter focuses largely on successful efforts to integrate learning with faith through the effective collaboration of scholars, administrators, donors, and students. Of course, the history of Christian higher education also contains countless cautionary tales. Well-known historical jeremiads by James Tunstead Burtchaell, George Marsden, and Mark Noll have carefully documented the way that board members, administrators, and faculty members all fall short of the glory of God in sustaining the faithful integration of learning.[41] But we need hope in these difficult times, which we may draw from the brighter lights in our collective history.

Higher education is always an expression of hope—most of all the hope that students can learn, that what they learn will make a difference for them and for others as they fulfill their callings into the future, and that beyond earning a livelihood they will lead meaningful lives. We need this hope both to meet the challenges of the present moment and for the future. Christian higher education always looks to a farther horizon, with hopes that reach for eternity. Scholarship is one of the many areas of life that—according to Jürgen Moltmann—brings "Christian hope and the promised future of God into the present day, and prepares the present day for this future."[42]

Marilynne Robinson draws a similar connection in *Gilead*, where she writes, "In eternity this world will be Troy, and all that has passed here will be the epic of the universe, the ballad they sing in the streets."[43] By

---

[40]Timothy Larsen, personal communication (August 2023).

[41]James Tunstead Burtchaell, *The Dying of the Light: The Disengagement of Colleges and Universities from Their Christian Churches* (Grand Rapids, MI: Eerdmans, 1998); George Marsden, *The Soul of the American University: From Protestant to Postsecular*, 2nd ed. (New York: Oxford University Press, 2021); Mark A. Noll, *The Scandal of the Evangelical Mind*, 2nd ed. (Grand Rapids, MI: Eerdmans, 2022).

[42]Jürgen Moltmann, *The Spirit of Hope: Theology for a World in Peril* (Louisville, KY: Westminster John Knox, 2019), 8.

[43]Marilynne Robinson, *Gilead* (New York: Farrar, Straus, & Giroux, 2004), 57.

referring to Troy, Robinson's words evoke the memory of *The Iliad* and *The Odyssey*—Homer's epic poems based on the Trojan Wars. The novelist is using core texts from the liberal arts tradition to cast daily life as an epic adventure. She is also suggesting that in the life to come the heroic deeds of this life will be remembered and celebrated. In some mysterious, beautiful way the things we learn and experience on earth are integral to our destiny.

Robinson's Christian hope is relevant for the life of faith and the pursuit of learning in God's everlasting kingdom. Christian education will find its grandest fulfillment in the life to come, when our highest hopes for the integration of faith and learning will prove to be eternal. In the meantime, the scholars, trustees, donors, and administrators who love to see learning flourish under the risen and ascended lordship of Jesus Christ will do everything possible to ensure that Christian higher education not only survives, but also strengthens future generations.

THREE

THE WAY OF WORDS

Conversation as a Hopeful
Educational Practice

Cherie Harder

CONVERSATION IS AND HAS EVER BEEN the bedrock of education and learning. From the moment we enter the world, we seek and respond to the words of others. Speech itself is learned in conversation, as babies respond to their parents by mirroring their sounds, words, and expressions. Toddlers navigate their expanding worlds by constantly asking "why?" From birth to death, the give-and-take of conversation helps cultivate curiosity, sharpen analysis, test logic, reveal new perspectives, enlarge the imagination, inspire empathy, and develop understanding.

So it is not surprising that the most renowned teachers of history taught largely through conversation. From Plato's 35 dialogues, to Jesus' teaching via parables and questions, to contemporary classroom Socratic discussions, the dynamic of conversation engages both student and teacher in intellectually challenging ways—requiring active listening, quick and accurate synthesis, and discerning responses. Such dialectic discussions also revealed and reinforced the connection to past conversations—what forebears had understood and argued and how it could be built upon or needed to be torn down. Indeed, the process of engaging seriously with the ideas of the past—affirming or amending them and wrestling with their implications for and claims on present understanding—has been called the Great Conversation.

In this chapter, I argue that conversation is not only a hopeful educational practice, but also a holistic and even holy one, a practice that not only transmits information and cultivates learning, but also forms one's imagination, intellect, and relationships, and, thus, one's character. We'll examine ways in which the practice of conversation has been distorted or degraded and discuss the potential for conversation to serve as a form of spiritual discipline, encouraging us to imitate Christ in our interactions and words. We'll also explore various ways and means of cultivating generative conversations.

CONVERSATION AS FORMATION

Conversation is not only about the exchange of information or opinion; it is necessarily relational and personal. To converse well with someone involves learning more about that person as well as the topic of the conversation. In conversation, we tell our stories, and we start to learn how and why others see the world the way they do. Even in a matter as basic as discussing a short story or poem, students realize that various interpretations emerge and that in sifting through them, one is often better equipped to refine one's own thinking and analysis.

In classroom conversation, students also learn to express themselves in relation to others, to make connections among information, ideas, and people. They learn to interpret texts and articulate their views, test their ideas against others' and critically weigh the text or presented argument, and potentially revise their own thinking based on input from others. They learn how deeply social their education is. Baylor humanities scholar Alan Jacobs noted in his wonderful book *How to Think*, "To think independently of other human beings is impossible, and if it were possible, it would be undesirable. Thinking is necessarily, thoroughly, and wonderfully social. Everything you think is a response to what someone else has thought and said."[1] None of us is truly an independent thinker. The way we think, what we think about, and the assumptions we make consist largely of what we have previously been exposed to through conversations.

As such, character as well as cognition are formed largely through conversation. Those with whom we engage in the most (and deepest) conversations will help shape imagination, empathy, and priorities. The way (or whether) we listen to others, respond to them, and express our thoughts are all morally formative, shaping us into the kind of person who attends to and cares for others—or doesn't. Learning to converse well opens possibilities for connection, wisdom, friendship, even justice. As Marilyn McEntyre wrote in her elegant work *Caring for Words in a Culture of Lies*:

> A large, almost sacramental sense of the import and efficacy of words can be found in early English usage, where conversation appears to have been a term that included and implied much more than it does now; to converse was to foster community, to commune with, to dwell in a place with others. Conversation was understood to be a life-sustaining practice, a blessing, and a craft to be cultivated for the common good.[2]

Quality conversations are not only vital to education; they are essential to a life well lived. This idea undergirds much of the work and mission of the Trinity Forum, which is dedicated to cultivating the best of Christian thought largely through conversation. When the Forum began decades ago, it focused on hosting Socratic conversations around "big questions"—the purpose of life, the formation of character, the meaning of leadership, or the nature of sin.

Those Socratic conversations would include a dozen or so couples who would gather for two or three days to discuss a selection of readings on a given topic. Moderators would keep the conversation going by asking open-ended questions and encouraging participants to respond to one another. The conversations often proved transformative. It was so

---

[1] Alan Jacobs, *How to Think* (New York: Currency, 2014), 37.
[2] Marilyn McEntyre, *Caring for Words in a Culture of Lies* (Grand Rapids, MI: Eerdmans, 2009), 2.

unusual for those participating to slow down, reflect on their experience, and wrestle with questions around meaning and purpose with others that many were moved to tears—and others to reassess their priorities. Some came to faith; some left their jobs. Many couples credited those weekends with strengthening, even saving, their marriages. They saw, and got to know, their spouses in a way that had been inaccessible before. By talking more deeply, they came to know and love each other more deeply as well.

At each forum, even when discussing the same written works presented to an earlier group, the conversation was unique. There was a different alchemy to each discussion, as each participant brought an individual perspective and experiential background to the table. New questions were asked, and explored, new stories told, and new possibilities considered. In his book *How to Know a Person*, columnist David Brooks described a great conversation as "an act of joint exploration" that "sparks you to have thoughts you never had before."[3] Such explorations illuminate new possibilities and reflect the purpose of education—to form as well as inform, to provide a travel guide to the good life.

Great conversations like this also deepen self-knowledge. Many forum participants later noted "aha" moments: they did not realize they thought something until they heard themselves saying it, almost always in response to someone else. Great conversations are a form of cartography; they map our interior lives as well as the landscape around us. And they beckon us deeper into previously unexplored internal territory.

As such, cultivating great conversations both inside and outside the classroom is both a source of joy and connection and a matter of serious importance. And the failure to do so has sobering consequences. Unfortunately, there is perhaps no educational practice that is more imperiled today than conversation.

CHALLENGES TO CONVERSATION AS EDUCATIONAL PRACTICE

Challenge of suppression/domination. The freedom to converse on various issues and ideas without repercussion or punishment is

---

[3]David Brooks, *How to Know a Person* (New York: Random House, 2023), 73.

increasingly threatened in academia. A recent study conducted by Heterodox Academy found that nearly two-thirds of students believed that the social and political climate at their college prevented students from speaking freely.[4] Another recent study conducted by the Foundation for Individual Rights and Expression (FIRE)[5] found that more than half of polled college professors are "shutting their mouths and biting their tongues"[6] due to fear of being reported, canceled, or even losing their jobs.

But while some students and teachers are self-censoring, others seem to deliberately distort the normal give-and-take of conversation into a battle for domination. In far too many schools, administrators police language and conversation; meanwhile, other students are allowed to use a "hecklers' veto" to drown out or threaten those saying things they don't want to hear. Whether shouting down speakers, disrupting classrooms, tearing down posters, or seeking to intimidate or "cancel" opponents, a minority of students—and faculty—have overtly sought not to engage with or even refute but, rather, to silence those with whom they disagree. Respected scholars and eager students alike are told that they have no business discussing issues or ideas that affect those of other demographic backgrounds with lower perceived power, that they "don't have standing" to speak or be listened to. Others are pressured to affirm and repeat ideological slogans or else their "silence is violence."

Challenge of social media. This negative symbiosis is further compounded by the medium through which so much of our public conversation is conducted.

As public discourse has increasingly moved into the virtual realm, our expectations and assumptions around the form and feel of conversations have also shifted. For most of us, in-person conversations are enhanced

---

[4]David Steele, "Afraid to Speak Up or Out," *Inside Higher Ed*, June 1, 2022, https://www.insidehighered .com/news/2022/06/02/survey-college-students-still-dont-feel-free-speak-campus.

[5]N. Honeycutt, S. T. Stevens, and E. Kaufmann, "The Academic Mind in 2022: What Faculty Think About Free Expression and Academic Freedom on Campus," The Foundation for Individual Rights and Expression, 2023, www.thefire.org/research-learn/academic-mind-2022-what-faculty -think-about-free-expression-and-academic-freedom.

[6]Rikki Schlott, "More Than Half of College Professors Bite Their Tongues over Cancel Culture Fears," February 28, 2023, https://nypost.com/2023/02/28/new-survey-reveals-college-professors -fear-of-being-canceled/.

by courtesy, reciprocity, clarity, and moderation. We like to talk with people who are thoughtful; we are less eager to converse with someone who yells, hurls insults, or spouts conspiracy theories.

As sensible as those preferences are, they are upended by social media. The kinds of interactions that social media fosters and rewards are markedly different from those cultivated in person and in classrooms. Social media measurably rewards snark, speed, hyperbole, and trolling (all corrosives to deep and meaningful in-person conversation) with attention, the currency of the online realm. It is the hot take, not thoughtful prudence or gracious forbearance, that garners likes, clicks, retweets, and comments. Across social media platforms (some more than others), a popular post has more currency than an accurate one, an insult generates more attention than a kind word; the extreme is more valued than the moderate. One MIT study found that falsehood spread six times more quickly on Twitter (now X) than accurate reporting.

Decades ago, when Marshall McLuhan declared that "the medium is the message," he was describing the way that our forms of communication shape the content and nature of our conversation. Years later, in his seminal work *Amusing Ourselves to Death*, sociologist Neil Postman tweaked McLuhan's argument by claiming "the medium is the metaphor"; that is, the communication medium we use biases us to see the world in a particular way, but often does so indirectly or allusively, so that we may not immediately recognize it as such. He noted in a speech summarizing the effects of technological change: "There is embedded in every great technology an epistemological, political, or social prejudice. Sometimes that bias is greatly to our advantage. Sometimes it is not. The printing press has annihilated the oral tradition; telegraphy has annihilated space; television has humiliated the word; the computer, perhaps, will degrade community life. And so on."[7]

Our great educational challenge is that the very technology we increasingly use for communication leaves us less eager and able to engage in quality conversations. In rewarding the speedy response over the

---

[7]Neil Postman, "Five Things We Need to Know About Technological Change" (speech delivered in Denver, CO, March 28, 1998, www.cs.ucdavis.edu/~rogaway/classes/188/materials/postman.pdf, 5).

thoughtful one, the sensational falsehood over the verified and understated, and tribalism over curiosity, we will inevitably encourage more of the former and less of the latter.

And as more of our public conversation moves online, the manners and mores of the virtual world have increasingly come to reflect and shape the norms of conversation offline and upend how we approach the act of conversation and our hopes for such interaction.

One particular challenge that social media poses to conversation writ large is the way the medium itself rewards contempt and nastiness.

The general speed, snark, snideness, and scapegoating encouraged by social media has increasingly characterized our conversational exchanges in general—with disastrous consequences. Not only does it (rather obviously) break down goodwill, trust, and cohesion, it also leaves us largely unable to understand one another. A recent study published in the *Journal of Computer-Mediated Communication* and reported in the *New York Times* and on NPR sought to study what was termed "the nasty effect"—the impact of insulting comments about an article on readers' capacity to accurately understand the article's content.[8] In the study, test subjects read an article making an argument about technology use. Some of the test subjects read comments which agreed or disagreed; some read comments that added insult and invective to disagreement. Simply reading the nasty comments, the researchers found, could significantly distort what the test subjects thought the original article reported. The authors noted: "Uncivil comments not only polarized readers, but they often changed a participant's interpretation of the news story itself. . . . Including an *ad hominem* attack in a reader comment was enough to make study participants think the downside of the purported technology was much greater than they'd previously thought."[9] In short, a nasty comment not only changed a reader's response to what was read; it changed his recollection and perception of it. Now imagine how much

---

[8]NPR *Talk of the Nation*, "The 'Nasty Effect': How Comments Color Comprehension," March 11, 2013, www.npr.org/2013/03/11/174027294/the-nasty-effect-how-comments-color-comprehension #:~:text=Now%20a%20study%20in%20the,the%20so%2Dcalled%20nasty%20effect.

[9]Dominique Brossard and Dietram A. Scheufele, "This Story Stinks," *New York Times*, March 2, 2013, www.nytimes.com/2013/03/03/opinion/sunday/this-story-stinks.html.

our ability to understand one another is taxed, given the toxic stew of invective and insult that characterizes so much of our online conversation! It is a wonder we understand one another at all.

CONVERSATION AS A CHRISTIAN PRACTICE

Despite the significant challenges, the pursuit of quality conversation is vital not only to education in general, but also to Christian education in particular. We worship the Word who spoke the world and all its diverse inhabitants into life and coexistence; as such, our creative act of conversation reflects the generativity of him whose image we bear. The trinitarian nature of God implies an eternal, joyful, and harmonious conversation between God the Father, Son, and Holy Spirit. The healing power of Jesus' words spoken to the sick, suffering, sinful, and spurned reflect the transformative potential of beholding and engaging with others. In a world created and sustained by a three-person God in perpetual conversation, the act of loving, truth-seeking, and generative conversation is not only a reflection of the divine, but also a means of grace and growth.

As the inimitable Eugene Peterson wrote in *The Jesus Way*:

> Words are holy—all words. . . .
>
> . . . Our language is derivative (as everything about us is!) from the language of God. Our common speech is in continuity with the language of God. Words are essential and words are holy wherever and whenever we use them. . . . We do well to reverence them, to be careful in our use of them, to be alarmed at their desecration, to take responsibility for using them accurately and prayerfully. Christian followers of Jesus have an urgent mandate to care for language—spoken, heard, or written—as a means by which God reveals himself to us, by which we express the truth and allegiance of our lives, and by which we give witness to the Word made flesh.[10]

CULTIVATING GENERATIVE CONVERSATIONS

So if conversation is both vital and imperiled, what steps might one take to encourage meaningful conversations? Here are a few suggestions on

---

[10]Eugene Peterson, *The Jesus Way* (Grand Rapids, MI: Eerdmans, 2007), 66-67.

basic but countercultural practices to encourage our formation as conversational creatures.

Keep it real. Prioritize face-to-face conversations over virtual interactions. Conversation in person is almost always deeper, more nuanced, and more connective than virtual exchanges. Simply being physically present changes conversation. As a corollary, it is often worth ignoring virtual exchanges with anonymous participants.

Give it time. Generative conversation requires time and space to develop and unfold. So often, our most meaningful conversations are those that unfolded over road trips or leisurely meals, or on vacation, when time is set aside and our interactions unhurried. Giving time to conversation is a countercultural act when there are so many incentives pushing us toward the rushed and transactional.

Listen. Listening well is a countercultural act. It means pushing back on social media incentives to stay in transmit mode, pushing pause on advancing our brand or agenda, and turning our full attention to another. Being fully and actively listened to is rare and remarkable. Many consultants or therapists encourage active listening. Others have promoted the idea of "loud listening"—vocalizing interest, agreement, or encouragement. Some experts emphasize "mirroring"—reflecting the postures and movement of the person you listen to as a form of empathic synchronization. Listening is, at its essence, an act of care, respect, and love. Henry David Thoreau once recalled that "the greatest compliment that was ever paid to me was when one asked me what I thought and attended to my answer."[11]

Listening is also rare. In her book *You're Not Listening,* Kate Murphy described interviewing people from a variety of ages, races, and socioeconomic backgrounds about listening. She recalled:

> Among the questions I asked was: who listens to you? Almost without exception, what followed was a pause. Hesitation. The lucky ones could come up with one or two people—usually a spouse or maybe a parent,

---

[11]Henry David Thoreau, *The Quotable Thoreau,* ed. Jeffrey S. Cramer (Princeton, NJ: Princeton University Press, 2011), 316.

best friend, or sibling. But many said, if they were honest, they didn't feel like they had anyone who truly listened to them, even those who were married or claimed a vast network of friends and colleagues. Others said they talked to therapists, life coaches, hairdressers, and even astrologers— that is, they paid to be listened to.[12]

Simply attending to the stories and ideas of another can help forge a connection and deepen one's thinking, whether or not one agrees with the substance of what is said. We learn and connect by listening, and in doing so, transform an exchange into an illumination.

Ask questions. A conversation without questions is merely a series of dueling transmissions (which is, in fact, much of social media communication). Inquiry opens up possibility. Done well, it requires attention, consideration, and understanding, such that the question apprehends what has been said and reforms it, whether through digging deeper, exploring what has been said, or extending the narrative or reasoning. Questions nourish and grow a conversation; a lack of questions starves it. But the art of asking questions is both undervalued and rarely practiced. In his delightful book *How to Know a Person,* David Brooks estimates that only around 30 percent of people are natural question askers; most of us simply don't think to do so. And yet, for most of us, we *love* to have questions asked of us. Brooks noted:

> I've come to think of questioning as a moral practice. When you are asking a good question, you are adopting a posture of humility. You are confessing that you don't know and you want to learn. You are also honoring a person. . . . The worst kinds of questions are the one that don't involve a surrender of power, that evaluate: where did you go to college? What neighborhood do you live in? What do you do? They imply, "I'm about to judge you." Closed questions are also bad questions. . . . Humble questions are open-ended. They're encouraging the other person to take control and take the conversation where they want it to go.[13]

---

[12]Kate Murphy, *You're Not Listening: What You're Missing and Why It Matters* (New York: Celadon Books, 2019), 17-18.

[13]Brooks, *How to Know,* 87-88.

He continued: "People are longing to be asked questions about who they are. . . . Each person is a mystery. And when you are surrounded by mysteries, as the saying goes, it's best to live life in the form of a question."[14] *Avoid invective and unnecessary provocation.* Insult will start a fight and end a conversation. Outsize provocation is almost always an attempt to embarrass, one-up, upset, or silence—which can easily incite a re-action, but rarely encourages conversation as a joint exploration. It also tends to drive people to dig further into their positions. In his book *Love Your Enemies*, Harvard Business School professor and economist Arthur Brooks describes the likely result of insult and provocation:

> Almost no one is ever insulted into agreement. . . . Research shows that insults actually intensify people's opposition to one's point of view. A classic 1967 study published in the *Journal of Experimental Social Psychology* "Negative Persuasion via Personal Insult," demonstrated what we call the "boomerang effect," a phenomenon that occurs when you insult somebody and, in doing so, cause them to harden their views. The re-searchers, from Yale University, showed that if people change their views at all, the odds are more than three-to-one that they will become more extreme in their original position.[15]

Scoring points at another's expense may feel good at the time, but it will kill the conversation and, with it, the likelihood of understanding, con-nection, or persuasion.

Ditch your phone. Phones are kryptonite to quality conversation. When our smartphones are nearby, we are distractable, if not fully dis-tracted. Our attention is divided between the virtual world and the em-bodied interactions in front of us, and the latter is the loser. In her book *You're Not Listening,* Kate Murphy described a University of Essex study that found

> the mere presence of a phone on the table—even if it's silent—makes those sitting around the table feel more disconnected and disinclined to talk about anything important or meaningful, knowing if they do, they will

---

[14]Brooks, *How to Know*, 93.
[15]Arthur Brooks, *Love Your Enemies* (New York: Broadside Books, 2019), 189-90.

probably be interrupted. It's a weird loop of the phone creating a circumstance where people will talk about things that aren't worth listening to, which in turn makes you more likely to stop listening and look at your phone.[16]

To dig deep, ditch the phone.

Read widely and well. Reading well enables conversing well. This may seem counterintuitive—after all, a book can't talk back and, in many cases, neither can the long-gone author. But reading requires consideration and interaction with a new perspective, an internal dialogue—even a willingness to empathically enter into the world of another to consider that person's foreign (and perhaps fictional) point of view. One learns to know one's own mind better in the process of apprehending another. And one begins to discover that one's thoughts are influenced by what one has previously read and discussed—and so are those of the very writers being read! Recognizing the ways in which various writers and thinkers are arguing with, imitating, building on, and responding to one another offers an implicit invitation to the reader to join in the exchange. It is the reason that engaging with the classics has been called the Great Conversation. Reading well is inherently dialectical. The habits of inquiry and curiosity nurtured by reading extend to embodied dialogue.

In addition to reading well, reading widely is also a boon to conversations that matter. Reading books from different time periods, places, and perspectives introduces us to a variety of perspectives and assumptions and forces us to engage with them. In his excellent work *Breaking Bread with the Dead,* Alan Jacobs argued that engaging with works from long ago and far away not only expands our world, but also leaves us more equipped and rooted in our own thought, conversations, and interactions. As he noted, "any significant increase in personal density is largely achieved through encounters with un-likeness." He explained his point in a recent Trinity Forum Online Conversation, saying:

> When you are engaged with the works of the past, you are dealing with difference. You are dealing with people whose whole world is different

---

[16]Murphy, *You're Not Listening*, 176.

than yours, people with different experiences, with a different outlook, with different ideas. You're doing so in an environment that you control. We all know how difficult it can be to try to maintain our patience. We certainly don't have any shot at serenity. We're just trying to maintain our patience when we're dealing with people who we strongly disagree with. But when it's the voices from the past, and we are visiting their world, and we assume the posture of visitors, of guests, then we can, I think, get a little bit of distance on our emotions. They're not going to talk back to us. They're not going to fight back. They're not going to do anything that will hurt us. If the encounter ends up being a little too intense for us, well, we can just close the book, and go away, and then come back to it later on when we've calmed down a little bit. It is training in encountering difference, but in a way that we have enough control over it, that it doesn't have to agitate us and frustrate us. But maybe if we do that for a while, we can get a little better at dealing with our immediate neighbors as well.[17]

Practice "epistemic humility." Epistemic humility—a reticence around certainty, an openness to adjusting one's point of view based on new information—can be an accelerant to the educational potency of conversation. Epistemic humility is not relativism. It does not at all deny the existence of truth but, rather, understands that one's personal understanding is inevitably limited or potentially distorted by one's own constraints, experiences, and predispositions. It encourages curiosity and a willingness to revise one's assumptions based on new information, which can encourage conversation as a joint exploration rather than debate.

Be mindful of interruptions. Energetic conversations between friends are often fast paced and informal and may include interruptions as they build on each other's thoughts. But often interruptions are a (perhaps subconscious) form of dominance assertion; as such, not surprisingly, they often feel disrespectful or dismissive to the person being interrupted. Conversations between people who do not know each other well that include a lot of interruptions (particularly if they are one sided) are more likely to build walls than build hope. Letting your conversational

---

[17]Trinity Forum, online conversation with Alan Jacobs, "Breaking Bread with the Dead," October 2, 2020, transcript, www.ttf.org/?portfolio=online-conversation-oct-2-alan-jacobs.

partner or participants finish their thought can give room to think and space for trust to build.

These are just a few possibilities for cultivating generative conversations. Brainstorming others would make for a great discussion! Asking colleagues, students, friends, and family members their thoughts on what makes for a great conversation—or to recount dynamics of important and educational conversations they've engaged in—will, in and of itself, generate insights and perhaps deepen connections.

Despite all the challenges to the practice of conversation in our time through the distortions of social media, the constraints on academic freedom, and the cruelties of a pervasive political and online culture that rewards the demeaning and dominating of others, the practice of conversation remains an inherently hopeful exercise—one that helps form our minds and relationships and opens new possibilities for understanding perspective, context, and motivation. But most significantly, the practice of conversation is ultimately an act of cocreation—a weaving of diffuse and different perspectives and ideas into something coherent, substantial, and meaningful. Ultimately, the hope and power of conversation lies in its reflection and re-creation of the generative work of the Word who spoke us into life—and speaks still.

FOUR

INCLUSIVE EXCELLENCE

Diversity as a Hopeful Educational Practice

KIMBERLY BATTLE-WALTERS DENU

FROM CHILDHOOD, I ROUTINELY noticed people others did not. Sensitive by nature and empathetic sometimes to a fault, I was drawn to the visibly invisible aspects of our social milieu and the obscure lived experiences of diverse groups of people. Perhaps that is why I became a sociologist, because I intuitively appreciated the importance of *noticing* and *looking again*, as "things aren't always as they appear."

Early in my teaching career, one of the great blessings I received was living in South Africa for part of a year as a Fulbright Scholar. During that season, I lived and taught in Johannesburg, was exposed to eleven official languages, and engaged a beautiful and vibrant people and country. It was incredible! It was also there that I had the serendipitous and surreal experience of staying in a guest house with the late Bishop Desmond Tutu and his lovely wife, Leah, while reading his book *No Future Without Forgiveness*.

While in South Africa, I also learned about the concepts of *sawubona* and *ubuntu*. The Zulu word *sawubona* is a greeting, analogous to hello, but its meaning is "I see you!" It is customary to bow when you say sawubona because you are acknowledging more than just a person's physical presence;

you are essentially saying, "I see your value and worth, the dignity of your humanity."[1] When I first learned the value of this practice, I was moved to tears. Why? Because as Oprah said at the end of her successful, twenty-five-year-running television show, after interviewing everyone from heads of state to street people, "At the end of the day, everyone wants to know—do you see me, do you hear me, and do I matter?" Everyone wants to matter. When we *see* people, they know they exist and have value.

The African word *ubuntu* is the concept "I am what I am because of who we all are."[2] Ubuntu suggests each person's value is based on the value of the whole. For Christians this value is steeped in the fact that we are the body of Christ and our collective value is connected to who we are as a whole, not as parts. We'll look at this more later in this chapter.

In this chapter, we will explore the value of *seeing* others, as well as our collective value and worth as fellow Christians. To help us do so, we will examine both sociological and biblical principles pertaining to diversity as a hopeful and essential practice within the academy, the church, and the broader community, as well as why I believe Christian higher education is best suited to speak into this important conversation for such a time as the one in which we find ourselves.

DIVERSITY TRENDS AND INCLUSIVE EXCELLENCE

A decade ago, for many Christian colleges, cultural diversity was aspirational. Today racial and ethnic diversity is no longer merely an aspirational goal but a realized part of the fabric of America and our campuses. In California, in addition to a growing number of other states, no one race or ethnic group makes up the majority of the population, thereby contributing to the rich milieu of multiculturalism.[3] According to US Census Bureau data, people of color, as a whole, will constitute the majority of the population in the United States by 2044, but non-Hispanic

---

[1] "Sawubona!," Loom International, August 7, 2020, www.loominternational.org/sawubona//.

[2] "The Story of Ubuntu," Canonical Ubuntu, https://ubuntu.com/about, accessed November 5, 2023; Nkem Ifejika, "What Does Ubuntu Really Mean?," *The Guardian*, September 28, 2006, www.theguardian.com/theguardian/2006/sep/29/features11.g2.

[3] Hans Johnson, Marisol Cuellar Mejia, and Eric McGhee, "California's Population," Public Policy Institute of California, January 2023 Fact Sheet, www.ppic.org/publication/californias-population/, accessed October 15, 2023.

Whites will still make up the single largest racial group of people.[4] While sociologist Richard Alba believes that the majority-minority demographic reports are misleading because they don't account for a large increase in the number of multiracial people (including mixed Whites), resulting in an overall decrease in the White population,[5] demographic data show that America is becoming more diverse.

For Christian higher education, much like the broader society, this will provide great opportunities and some foreseeable challenges for which we have the privilege and responsibility to prepare our graduates. The Council for Christian Colleges and Universities (CCCU) recently reported an increase in diversity within its member campuses over the past decade. Today more than 30 percent of all students who attend CCCU institutions are students of color.[6] But why does this matter? This matters because people matter. Today we use the phrase *inclusive excellence* to encapsulate the value of diversity in the learning environment. In other words, if our campuses welcome some students but inadvertently exclude others, we haven't truly become an excellent community.

Inclusive excellence measures an institution's success and prestige not only by its academic accolades, but also by how well it values and engages its members from diverse backgrounds, as well as its intentionality with regard to its comprehensive integration of diversity within academic life. Inclusive excellence integrates a holistic approach to diversity in academic settings and includes diverse pedagogy and curricula, cultural awareness, becoming a welcoming and respectful community, and culturally inclusive policies and practices.[7] Some documented benefits of

---

[4]Jonathan Vespa, Lauren Medina, and David M. Armstrong, "Demographic Turning Points for the United States: Population Projections for 2020 to 2060," U.S. Census, February 2020, www .census.gov/content/dam/Census/library/publications/2020/demo/p25-1144.pdf.

[5]Richard Alba, "What Majority-Minority Society? A Critical Analysis of the Census Bureau's Projections of America's Demographic Future," *Socius* 4: 1-10.

[6]Council for Christian Colleges and Universities, "Diversity on CCCU Campuses," January 2021, diversity.cccu.org/wp-content/uploads/2021/01/2021-CCCU-Diversity-Stats.pdf; Nathan Grawe, "Changing Demographics and the Agile College," Council for Christian Colleges and Universities online magazine, Spring 2022, www.cccu.org/magazine/changing-demographics-agile-college/.

[7]"Resources to Support Inclusivity in the Classroom," University of Denver Office of Teaching & Learning Inclusive Teaching Practices, https://operations.du.edu/inclusive-teaching, accessed November 5, 2023.

inclusive excellence include improved academic outcomes, greater problem-solving and innovation, a reduction in the perpetuation of segregation across races, and higher levels of civic engagement.[8]

SOCIOLOGICAL PERSPECTIVES OF DIVERSITY

Sociology is the study of human social interactions, including the observation of social change, the examination of social conflict, and the study of cultural patterns and phenomena. Three central sociological perspectives provide a foundation for social understandings, including our look at diversity: the functionalist perspective, conflict theory, and symbolic interaction.

Functionalist perspective. The functionalist perspective, largely attributed to Talcott Parsons and Robert Merton, looks at society analogous to a machine with many parts. The parts work together for the functioning of the whole. In addition to people, some examples of parts include societal norms and cultural values that help shape individual behaviors and minimize outliers or extremes.[9]

From a functionalist's perspective, as a nation of immigrants we are better and stronger because immigrants bring many things to our nation, including intellectual vigor and innovation, a strong work ethic and grit, an appreciation for education, and a willingness to take entry-level jobs that many citizens will not. But the functionalist's perspective would also suggest that the United States has basic values and norms that a culturally pluralistic nation like the United States accepts and lives by. Many of these values are engrained in our constitution and mores.

For example, freedom of religion, freedom to express oneself through speech, independence, and so forth—these values, norms, and traditions are practiced daily and reinforced within the tapestry of the larger social fabric. When something or someone threatens these values, cultural

---

[8]J. F. Milem, "The Educational Benefits of Diversity: Evidence from Multiple Sectors," in *Compelling Interest: Examining the Evidence on Racial Dynamics in Higher Education*, ed. M. Chang, D. Witt, J. Jones, and K. Hakuta (Stanford, CA: Stanford University Press, 2003), 126-69.

[9]Doyle Paul Johnson, *Sociological Theory: Classical Founders and Contemporary Perspectives* (New York: John Wiley & Sons, 1981), 385-440.

mechanisms work to move them back in place, as evident through public demonstrations, protests, and our voting process.

To add to this point, the strengths perspective,[10] which focuses on the strengths and resourcefulness of something, instead of the pathologies, would also suggest that diversity across race and ethnicity, in addition to other forms of diversity, adds to our pulchritudinous population, promotes multilingual practices, provides opportunities to learn different customs and traditions, and enhances our ability to value differences.

Another function of diversity is its impact on our ability to foster cultural awareness and competence and cultural humility. Cultural awareness and cultural competence are tools that foster the understanding that the world is not monolithic and not everyone sees or understands the world in the same way. In Christian higher education, an obligation to educate and prepare students to understand, engage, and successfully live in a pluralistic society is critical.

Fortunately, Christian colleges are well poised to follow through on these commitments. We get the opportunity to help our students serve God, others, and the church by helping them first understand the broader culture in which they live. Some of the ways we do this is by offering off-campus programs in both urban and international settings; providing service learning opportunities within underprivileged and diverse communities; and encouraging our students to study and learn foreign languages. Through intentional practices, students journey toward cultural understanding and humility and a life of service.

Conflict theory. Conflict theory is largely attributed to Karl Marx and examines dissonance and competition within the social milieu for power, distributions of resources, and the impetuses for social change that can lead to new and holistic stability.[11] Conflict theory allows us to examine tensions pertaining to the perceived paucity of *power* (political, positional, access), *resources* (money, privileges, assets), and equitable *policies* (laws, rules, actions).

---

[10]Dennis Saleeby, ed., *The Strengths Perspective in Social Work Practice*, 2nd ed. (White Plains, NY: Longman, 1997).
[11]Johnson, *Sociological Theory*, 447-501.

When it comes to diversity, several scholars have looked through the lens of the conflict perspective when examining systemic issues pertaining to inequalities, injustices, and the roots of racism. In his book *America's Original Sin*, author and minister Jim Wallis says, "Racism is rooted in sin . . . which goes deeper than politics, pointing fingers . . . blaming, or name calling."[12] He goes on to note that racism is steeped in greed, a lust for power, and the bold move for dominance. According to Wallis, racism isn't about *good* people versus *bad*, or even relegated to individuals, but about unjust systems and practices, including ones with a history of documented inequities toward people of color: the legal system, the GI Bill, home loans, health care gaps, and educational disparities. According to Wallis, we can't say we're not racist if we accept and support systems that are.[13]

As a White man, Wallis writes that racism is not just a problem for people of color but for Whites, who must be a part of the solution. He goes on to say, "White people in the United States have benefited from the structures of racism. . . . And if whites have profited from a racist system, we must change it."[14] Quoting Martin Luther King Jr., Wallis isn't looking for "an eye for an eye or a tooth for a tooth, thereby leaving everyone blind and toothless as a nation," but, rather, for moral leadership that will act as a compass to help navigate demographic changes while building community and minimizing collisions.[15]

Challenging the status quo, Ibram Kendi, in his book *How to Be an Antiracist*, states the opposite of racism is not nonracism but antiracism. According to Kendi, no neutral space exists. He then writes there are basically three responses to racism: we ignore it; we copy it; or we eliminate it. Kendi proposes action, suggesting that we actively engage in dismantling racist policies and the misuse of power that normalize systemic inequities.

In *Embrace: God's Radical Shalom for a Divided World*, pastor and author Leroy Barber offers that fear is at the root of conflict. Taking a gospel-centered approach within the conflict perspective, Barber

---

[12]Jim Wallis, *America's Original Sin* (Grand Rapids, MI: Brazos, 2016), 33.
[13]Wallis, *America's Original Sin*, 32.
[14]Wallis, *America's Original Sin*, 49.
[15]Wallis, *America's Original Sin*, 135, 189.

advocates for engaging others who are different from ourselves. Barber offers ways to engage across differences such as reading books written by people of color, moving beyond our comfort zones to attend an ethnic church other than our own, and participating in diverse community events. Barber says that God doesn't prioritize our comfort. This is not about comfort; rather, relationships save us from prioritizing our own comfort to the detriment of others.[16]

Barber also helps us understand the Black Lives Matter movement. He explains that the movement is essentially saying that Black Lives Matter *too*—speaking both to Black people as well as others, especially following a plethora of high-profile police brutality and murder cases within Black communities.

As a person who loves peace, I reflect on the question, "Is it possible to have community without conflict?" Perhaps others may disagree with me, but I don't think it's possible this side of heaven. Why? Because we are all broken, flawed, and often operate out of our own selfish ambitions. Although very few of us like conflict, we must not avoid it or resist it out of fear or to contrive peace. Why? Conflict can open our eyes to problems, which can be the impetus for deeper conversations and new understandings, ultimately leading us to address critical issues that make us better.

For example, just look at our personal relationships. We have conflicts with the people we love, understand, and extend grace to the most. Nevertheless, this does not prevent us from continuing to show up and working through those conflicts. In fact, this is what we celebrate—*the good stuff*—persistence, grit, and never giving up. This is why we love to celebrate the fiftieth wedding anniversary of a couple, the retirement of a person's protracted and beautiful career, or healthy parent-child relationships with one's adult children. None of the stories leading to these moments are devoid of conflict, but they represent working through the conflict to get to the other side of it to a beautiful life that reflects that we didn't give up. When it comes to diversity, we must do the same—keep coming to the table, persist, and never give up. Is it hard? Yes. Is it worth it? Definitely!

---

[16]Leroy Barber, *Embrace: God's Radical Shalom for a Divided World* (Downers Grove, IL: InterVarsity Press, 2016), 131.

Symbolic interaction. Largely associated with George Herbert Mead, Charles Horton Cooley, and Erving Goffman, symbolic interaction looks at the meanings that humans ascribe to symbols, circumstances, or events, and how individuals negotiate those shared meanings and interpretations.[17] Two relevant but very different examples of symbols that have had negative meanings associated with them are: Christian nationalism and critical race theory (CRT). In this section we will explore both.

First, Christian nationalism is an amalgamation of Christianity, nationalism, and politics. Pushing beyond patriotism, it seeks to hold onto an ideal of America from a nostalgic past, that wasn't (and still isn't) always favorable to "outsiders," including people of color, immigrants, those from different political parties, and non-Christians. When describing Christian nationalism, one Christian scholar said, "Christianity becomes a fig leaf to cover political programming and propaganda."[18]

In *American Idolatry: How Christian Nationalism Betrays the Gospel and Threatens the Church*, sociologist Andrew Whitehead examines the problems associated with the conflation of religious, political, and sometimes racist symbols. He discusses how within Christian nationalism differences are often seen as dangerous, causing some Christians to "otherize" those we disagree with or who "don't fit in." He contends a perceived loss of privilege and power is what Christian nationalists believe they must fiercely protect.

The insurrection that unfolded at the Capitol in Washington, DC, on January 6, 2021, is one example of this. Christian nationalists believed it was their duty to take back what was theirs and to fight to overturn the election results. According to Whitehead, there are three idols of Christian nationalism: power, fear, and violence. Although power and privilege are seen as things that need to be protected among Christian nationalists, fear and violence are often used as tools to help ensure the nondisturbance of power and privilege.

---

[17]Johnson, *Sociological Theory*, 291-336.
[18]Paul D. Miller, "What Is Christian Nationalism?," *Christianity Today*, February 3, 2021, www .christianitytoday.com/ct/2021/february-web-only/what-is-christian-nationalism.html.

On January 6, symbols of flags and crosses were visible alongside racist symbols of violence and death, such as nooses. Some Americans saw the insurrection as a moment of pride, protecting *their* America; others watched in horror, internalizing the violence that implied that they did not belong, were not welcome in *this* America, and could be harmed. While some wore hats with the abbreviation MAGA (Make America Great Again), some read and interpreted that as Make America *White* Again, a fear response and backlash to changing demographics, and a blatant takeback move on the heels of the first elected Black president. Here symbolic interactionism illuminates how one symbol can have multiple meanings depending on one's social location in society.

Second, CRT has become associated with dangerous rhetoric, believed by some to be anti-White, and banned from some schools and scrutinized in some colleges. Before we look at this further, it is important to note that CRT is not one theory but a broad framework used to understand racial matters within the context of systems. In his article "What Christians Get Wrong About Critical Race Theory," Nathan Luis Cartagena highlights this point, going on to note that CRT is a framework that reviews and critiques systems and practices that negatively affect race and people from diverse backgrounds.[19] Cartagena notes that the framework must be viewed through an antiracist lens. It helps us understand structures of subordination and suppression, while encouraging us to change them. His thesis is that Christians must seek to understand and assess CRT rather than simply dismiss it; in addition, he admonishes us to review history honestly. Although he acknowledges that race is socially constructed, he recognizes that we live in a racialized society that has real consequences, especially for people of color.

In my book *Sheila's Shop*, I discuss the "cumulative lived experiences" of working-class Black women. In addition to chronicling what sociologists would call *micro-* and *macro*aggressions, which were experienced frequently by these women through verbal and nonverbal symbols and actions, I highlighted what I call "racial and gender victorization," which

---

[19]Nathan Luis Cartagena, "What Christians Get Wrong About Critical Race Theory—Part 1," *Faithfully*, February 27, 2020, https://faithfullymagazine.com/critical-race-theory-christians/.

enabled them to live in a place of resilience, joy, and hope, despite systemic issues centered on race, class, and gender matters.[20] The words of Will Foley perfectly encapsulate their lived experiences: "The world is full of cactus, but we don't have to sit on it."[21] These women experienced the same inequalities and injustices as other people of color, yet they refused to see themselves as victims. This did not mean they passively accepted a subpar fate, but that they did what they needed to do and didn't allow negative circumstances outside of their control to dictate their lived experiences.

While this section has used a social science lens to review diversity, specifically race and ethnicity, the following section will examine diversity from a biblical lens.

Koinonia: Biblical Bases for Diversity

One of the first Bible verses that many of us learn as children is John 3:16: "For God so loved the world that he gave his one and only Son, that whoever believes in him shall not perish but have eternal life" (NIV). Growing up in the Black church, I remember hearing my grandfather, who was also my pastor, emphasize that God loved *the world*. Perhaps he intentionally stressed the word *world* to ensure that we knew that God's love was limitless. Or perhaps it was to underscore that everyone was included. Regardless of his intentions, as a little girl and now an adult, I took both meanings to heart.

Diversity was God's plan and idea long before it became ours. Throughout Scripture we see the abundant diversity of God's creation— from plants and terrain to animals and humankind—God said it was good. God could have made one of each thing but all of nature points to God's boundless creativity and love of diversity. Revelation 7:9 describes a great multitude of people standing before the throne of God from "all nations, tribes, peoples, and tongues" (NKJV). Even as John 3 declares that God loves the world, Revelation 7 depicts the world standing before God's throne, grafted into God's family through Christ, God's Son.

---

[20]Kimberly Battle-Walters, *Sheila's Shop: Working-Class African American Women Talk About Life, Love, Race, and Hair* (Lanham, MD: Rowman & Littlefield, 2004).

[21]Will Foley, as quoted in Paul Brownlow, *Little Bits of Wisdom* (1995), as noted in Battle-Walters, *Sheila's Shop*, 105.

When Scripture describes the body of Christ (1 Cor 12:12-27), it does so by describing the various parts while underscoring their essential functions for the good of the whole. No one part is more important than the other. Each is vital. The Greek word *koinonia* is defined as "Christian fellowship or body of believers; intimate spiritual communion and participative sharing in a common religious commitment and spiritual community."[22] As individuals, we come with our differences, adding to the larger community, bringing both complexity and beauty for the glory of God. Galatians 3:28 says, "There is neither Jew nor Greek, there is neither slave nor free, there is neither male nor female; for you are all one in Christ Jesus" (NKJV). Although we are diverse by race, gender, nationality, and social class, we are part of the body of Christ, the church. For Christians, our common denominator is Jesus Christ. Our redemption and hope are found in Christ alone, not in our beautiful but temporal human identities lest we turn them into idols. Does this mean that we should forsake our individuality or our ethnic heritage in our push for a more just world? No. But it does suggest that we not lose sight of our ultimate identity as children of God, working together in love, understanding that the ultimate "righting" of every wrong happens in heaven.

In his work, philosopher and theologian Nicholas Wolterstorff challenges us to restore and have right relationships with God, humanity, nature, and ourselves. According to Wolterstorff, justice is the ground floor of shalom, providing the foundation for human flourishing.[23] Part of the work of diversity is to bring us into right relationship with God, others, nature, and ourselves. What would it look like to promote the flourishing of all people, "Thy kingdom come, thy will be done, on earth, *as it is in heaven*"? We are invited to partner with God to repair the world, through activities such as creation care and social justice, knowing that full restoration is in Christ alone. As followers of Christ, as the blessed "peacemakers," we get to declare and pursue peace—shalom—wherever we go.

---

[22]Merriam-Webster, s.v. *koinonia*, accessed February 10, 2024, www.merriam-webster.com/dictionary/koinonia#:~:text=1,other%20and%20with%20their%20Lord.

[23]Nicholas Wolterstorff, *Educating for Shalom: Essays on Christian Higher Education* (Grand Rapids, MI: Eerdmans, 2004).

Looking forward by looking back. In Martin Luther King Jr.'s final book, *Where Do We Go from Here?*, King asks if the United States will move toward chaos or community. He outlines his dreams for America's future, including the need to address real global and domestic issues, but through the eyes of hope. Rev. King's message of hope is still vibrant and relevant today in both Christian higher education and in the United States.

Psalm 39:7 says, "And now, Lord, what do I wait for? My hope is in You" (NKJV). The Hebrew word for *hope, qavah*, means waiting with expectations.[24] For Christians, our hope is based on Jesus' life, death, and resurrection rather than *our* works, optimism, or activism. This does not mean that Christians should remain silent or be passive in the face of injustice, but that our hopeful outlook and advocacy for diversity is not dependent on us alone. We have a greater hope in Christ.

The greatest commandment and great commission. In Mark 12:30-31, when a scribe asks Jesus what the most important commandment of all is, Jesus replies, "And you shall love the Lord your God with all your heart and with all your soul and with all your mind and with all your strength." He goes on to say that the second greatest commandment is to "love your neighbor as yourself" (ESV). The call to diversity in higher education is ultimately a call to love our neighbors as ourselves. This call is to live in proximity with our neighbors, which means to do life with them, even when we experience conflict, disagreements, or see and value things differently. Scripture goes on to say that Christians will be known by their love (Jn 13:35).

What makes the practice of diversity in Christian higher education more effective and shoulders above secular models is that love and human flourishing are at the heart of it—right relationship with God, others, and ourselves. As Wolterstorff noted, biblical justice is the foundation for that love and peace, which ultimately seeks restoration and reconciliation. This love is a bridge over racial chasms and strained conversations and a pathway through the labyrinth of cultural wars. If we say we love God, that love must be evident in how we love and listen to our neighbors, including those who speak other languages, vote differently,

---

[24]The Bible Project Bible App, "Qavah," discussed by Tim Mackie, October 22, 2023, devotional.

and look and live differently than us. Once we have loved well, we gain the opportunity to witness well (Great Commission). Imagine, just for a minute, that the *greatest commandment* and the *Great Commission* were meant to go hand in hand: love first, share (the faith) second.

Love in Practice: "When You Pray, Move Your Feet"—African Proverb

I was once told that love is not an emotion but an action that is put into practice. Real love leads to action. One very practical way our college decided to put love for our neighbor into action is through a new general education requirement for all incoming students called Justice, Reconciliation, and Diversity on Biblical and Theological Grounds. In select courses, students grapple with matters surrounding race and ethnicity in the United States and beyond, examine historical hegemony, and learn biblical understandings of justice. They address what I call *glomestic diversity*—how domestic and global matters intertwine. They also take a deeper look at the role that "exoticism" plays in making us romanticize international issues yet bypass similar matters on domestic soil.

God-honoring diversity is not accidental but intentional. Our goal is to prepare our graduates for a pluralistic world, to work well alongside differences, and to love both Christ and their neighbor so well that they will be known for this love, thereby leading others to it. By instituting this learning requirement, we teach our students that love is an action that must be practiced daily.

Shirley Hoogstra, president of the CCCU, noted that "we have the great and difficult privilege of representing God's kingdom," yet she is convinced that our transformative gospel from sin and failure to grace and love positions us to model and lead these crucial discussions.[25] Despite the challenges, difficulties, and patience it takes to do this well—I wholeheartedly agree.

---

[25]In Karen Longman, ed., *Diversity Matters: Race, Ethnicity, and the Future of Christian Higher Education* (Abilene, TX: Abilene Christian University Press, 2017).

—FIVE—

READING FOR DEIFICATION

Maximus the Confessor's Hopeful Pedagogy

Hans Boersma

In the beginning was the Word. Reading begins with the Word and ends with the Word. In this chapter, I focus on three particular "books" meant to be read, namely, the Word as made present in Christ, in creation, and in Scripture—asking the question: How does their reading offer hope? All three books have their origin in the Logos, and all three take us back into the Logos. Put differently, embodied words are key to the expanding (*diastellein*) or unfolding (*explicatio*) of the Logos and to the contracting (*systellein*) or enfolding (*complicatio*) back into the Logos.[1]

We do our reading, therefore, within the temporal fold where the Logos thickens into human words. Reading is an inherently hopeful

---

[1] As we will see below, the language of *diastellein* and *systellein* comes from Saint Maximus the Confessor. Nicholas of Cusa used the words *explicatio* and *complicatio* to denote this same *exitus* and *reditus*. For Cusa's theology of *exitus* and *reditus*, see Nancy J. Hudson, "Divine Immanence: Nicholas of Cusa's Understanding of Theophany and the Retrieval of a 'New' Model of God," *Journal of Theological Studies* NS 56 (2005): 250-70; Knut Alfsvåg, "Explicatio and Complicatio: On the Understanding of the Relationship Between God and the World in the Work of Nicholas Cusanus," *International Journal of Systematic Theology* 14 (2012): 295-309; and Catherine Keller, "Enfolding and Unfolding God: Cusanic Complicatio," in *Cloud of the Impossible: Negative Theology and Planetary Entanglement* (New York: Columbia University Press, 2014), 87-124.

practice, grounded in the recognition that Christ, creation, and Scripture are rational expansions of the Logos—books of God, through the reading of which we, too, are contracted or enfolded into the Logos, who himself is the rational expression of the Father. *Reading offers hope because it is the practice through which we enter into the eternal Word of God.*

Let me first, however, enter an important caveat: reading is not ultimate, for it takes place only within the fold that marks the unfolding from the Logos and the enfolding back into the Logos. Reading stems from silence, and it ends in silence. Lectio divina, the traditional monastic practice of biblical reading, meditation, prayer, and contemplation, is not only interspersed with periods of silence, but it also begins and ends with silence.[2] The silence preceding and following the reading of lectio divina betokens the silence of the God who, inasmuch as he is beyond being (*hyperousios*), is also beyond speech (*arrētos*) and hence unknowable (*agnōstos*). The processes of expansion and contraction involve, respectively, the gift of speech and the consummation of speech. The Logos himself is beyond being and thought, and our aim in the reading of the three books is to be united with the Logos beyond created discourse. Reading, therefore, is a practice that characterizes our world of time and space, a practice that (1) takes place in a world where the Logos has expanded (*diastellein*) or unfolded (*explicatio*) into the multiplicity of this-worldly being and (2) contracts (*systellein*) or enfolds (*complicatio*) us into the Logos of God.[3]

Silence—that which precedes and follows all our reading—characterizes, therefore, the beginning and the end, the Alpha and the Omega, whence we have come and whither we return.[4] Paradise, the place of our

---

[2]See my discussion in *Pierced by Love: Divine Reading with the Christian Tradition* (Bellingham, WA: Lexham Press, 2023), 181-202.

[3]In what follows, I will focus on our reading of the Logos as embodied in Christ, creation, and Scripture. The underlying assumption of the close relationship between nature and the supernatural means that whatever claim I make about the reading of these three books has implications for *all* reading—since all human words participate, in their own distinct manner, in the eternal Logos of God.

[4]Robert Cardinal Sarah comments, "The silence of eternity is the consequence of God's infinite love. In heaven, we will be with Jesus, totally possessed by God and under the influence of the Holy Spirit. Man will no longer be capable of saying a single word. Prayer itself will have become impossible. It will become contemplation, a look of love and adoration. The Holy Spirit will inflame the souls who go to heaven. They will be completely given over to the Spirit." Robert

origin and destiny, does not have letters, syllables, and words the way we know them. The Word of God (*verbum Dei*) is also, at one and the same time, the Silence of God (*silentium Dei*), for the Son of God is beyond this-worldly human words. In him, human words find their telos—both in that he is their aim and that they cease in him in paradise—transfigured as they are in the logoi of the Logos.

THE BASIS FOR READING: LOGOS AND LOGOI

Saint Maximus the Confessor (ca. 580–662) dwells at length on the relationship between the Logos and the logoi in his *Ambigua*, written ca. 628 to John, archbishop of Cyzicus. He does so most elaborately and famously in *Ambiguum 7*. Drawing on Dionysius's *The Divine Names*, Maximus here explains the logoi as being similar (though by no means identical) to Plato's forms or ideas (*ambig.* 7.24; cf. *qu. Thal.* 13.2).[5] Maximus writes that the Logos of God, from all eternity,

> contained within Himself the preexisting logoi of created beings. When, in His goodwill, He [i.e., God the Father] formed out of nothing [*ek tou mē*] the substance of the visible and invisible worlds, He did so on the basis of these logoi. By His *word (logos) and His wisdom He created* and continues to create *all things* [cf. Wis. 9:1–2]—universals [*ta katholou*] as well as particulars [*ta kath' hekaston*]—at the appropriate time. We believe, for example, that a logos of angels preceded and guided their creation; and the same holds true for each of the *beings and powers* [cf. 1 Pet. 3:22] that

---

Cardinal Sarah with Nicolas Diat, *The Power of Silence: Against the Dictatorship of Noise*, trans. Michael Miller (San Francisco: Ignatius, 2017), 98.

[5] I am using Maximus the Confessor, *On Difficulties in the Church Fathers: The Ambigua*, 2 vols., trans. and ed. Nicholas Constas, Dumbarton Oaks Medieval Library 28-29 (Cambridge, MA: Harvard University Press, 2014), abbreviated as *ambig.*; and Maximus the Confessor, *On Difficulties in Sacred Scripture: The Responses to Thalassios*, trans. Maximos Constas, Fathers of the Church 136 (Washington, DC: Catholic University of America Press, 2018), abbreviated as *qu. Thal.* For Dionysius's brief mentioning of the logoi, see *The Divine Names* 5.8 (PG 3.824C). Adam G. Cooper comments that the logoi "seem akin to what Aristotelian philosophy means by natures or forms. They are a limit concept, answering the question: what kind of thing is that? A thing's *logos* defines its basic what and wherefore, its essence and purpose, in relation to itself, to other beings and to God. . . . It can also function as a kind of natural law, telling us in general terms what a thing *should* be, how it should (or should not) *act* relative to its God-given nature and design, even if for one reason or another it may in fact deviate from this 'natural' course." "Spiritual Anthropology in *Ambiguum 7*," in *The Oxford Handbook of Maximus the Confessor*, ed. Pauline Allen and Bronwen Neil (New York: Oxford University Press, 2015), 365.

fill the world above us. A logos of human beings likewise preceded their creation, and—in order not to speak of particulars—a logos preceded the creation of everything that has received its being from God. (*ambig. 7.16*)[6]

This description closely links the preexisting logoi of created beings—angels, humans, and all created things—with the eternal Word or Logos of God. Maximus believed that the Creator-creature relationship is grounded in the eternal logoi, which together make up the one Logos of God, asserting straightforwardly that "the many logoi are one Logos" (7.15).[7] When dealing with the logoi, Maximus's focus is squarely on the ultimate source of God's activity in the world, namely, the beyond-being (*hyperousios*) triune God—in particular, the Logos as the second person of the Trinity. Torstein Tollefsen defines Maximus's logoi as follows: they are "God's intentions through which all creatures receive their generic, specific, and individual essences. The *logoi* are acts of will instituting essence."[8] This description implies that the logoi are a particular kind of activity or *energeia* in God. As Tollefsen puts it: "Even if all the *logoi* are activities of the divine will, all divine activities in the broader sense are not *logoi*."[9]

The Confessor distinguishes the logoi sharply from creaturely beings, both particulars *and* universals. After all, as we just saw, he writes that

---

[6]Commenting on this passage and on *qu. Thal.* 48, Jordan Daniel Wood comments, "Maximus is clear that an individual's *logos* establishes its simultaneous unified participation in many levels of being, from its species to its highest genera ('common being'): in the concrete individual are wrought 'many and sundry unifications of things separated,' like many 'angels' converging at a single point." "Creation Is Incarnation: The Metaphysical Peculiarity of the *logoi* in Maximus Confessor," *Modern Theology* 34 (2018): 87n27.

[7]Cf. Maximus's elaboration on this in *ambig.* 7.20. Maximus is similar to Plotinus, for whom the intellect (*nous*) wills the logoi (*Enneads* 6.2.21). Maximus moves beyond Plotinus, however, by identifying the Logos (along with the logoi) with the One. As Wood rightly points out, for Christians (including Maximus), God himself is the principle that constitutes the one Logos and the many logoi. "Creation Is Incarnation," 90.

[8]Torstein Theodor Tollefsen, *The Christocentric Cosmology of St. Maximus the Confessor* (New York: Oxford University Press, 2008), 170. Cf. David Bradshaw's comment: "It would be a mistake to think of them [i.e., the logoi] simply as intelligible contents or individual essences. They are the purposes that God has in creating things, and, consequently, the meanings that these things have within the divine mind." *Aristotle East and West: Metaphysics and the Division of Christendom* (Cambridge: Cambridge University Press, 2004), 205. Andrew Louth similarly suggests that the "*logoi*, according to which we are created, are precisely God's will and predetermination for each creature. They are not 'things', ontic realities; they are what God intends for each of his creatures." "St Maximos' Doctrine of the *Logoi* of Creation," *Studia Patristica* 48 (2010): 82.

[9]Tollefsen, *Christocentric Cosmology*, 171.

the Father created all things—"universals (*ta katholou*) as well as particulars (*ta kath' hekaston*)"—out of nothing through his Logos. When he speaks of "universals," Maximus seems to have in mind the larger units of species and genera that contain particulars; he places both these universals and particulars on the level of created, this-worldly being.[10] Whereas Plato had treated universals as eternal ideas, Maximus places universals on the creaturely side of things. As a result, the logoi, for him, are not universals but are the predetermining intentions or wills contained within the eternal Word of God. Maximus, we could also say, Christianizes Plato by suggesting that created things (universals and particulars) are the product of God, created according to their eternal logoi or ideas.

The Possibility of Reading: The Logos Embodied

In Maximus's view, the Logos, who as the second person of the Trinity is absolutely simple, "becomes thick" (*pachynthēnai*) or "embodies" (*sōmatōthēnai*) himself in three ways: in the incarnation; in creation; and in Scripture. Each form of embodiment has to do with education and with words (logoi). The first "thickening" of the Logos, explains Maximus, is his "manifestation" (*parousia*) in the flesh of Christ (*ambig.* 33.2). Its purpose was explicitly pedagogical, namely,

> that He might instruct [*ekthesthai didaskalian*] us, by means of words [*phōnais*] and examples [*paradeigmasi*] suited to us, in mysteries [*aporrētōn*] that transcend the power of all human speech [*logou*]. (*For we know that all that He said was in the form of parables, and that He said nothing without a parable* [Matt. 13:34], for teachers [*didaskalois*] typically have recourse to parables whenever their pupils [*akroatai*] are not immediately able to follow them, and so endeavor to lead them to an understanding of what is being said.) (*ambig.* 33.2)

---

[10]Following the fourth-century Christian philosopher Nemesius, Maximus insists that universals come and go with the particulars in which they manifest themselves: "If the universals [*katholou*] subsist in the particulars [*tois kata meros*], and do not in any way possess their principle [*logon*] of being and existence by themselves, then it is quite clear that, if the particulars [*kata meros*] were to disappear, the corresponding universals (*katholou*) would cease to exist. For the parts [*merē*] exist and subsist in the wholes [*holotēsi*], and the wholes [*holotētes*] in the parts [*meresi*], and no argument can refute this" (*ambig.* 10.101; cf. 41.10).

Maximus's language is pedagogical throughout. The Logos became incarnate in Christ with the distinct purpose of serving as our teacher through words and examples by way of parables and so leading us into the ineffable secrets or mysteries (*aporrētoi*) that transcend human speech (*logos*). The Word became flesh so that by words he might lead us into the ineffable Word beyond words.[11] In short, we witness the first embodiment of the Logos, that of the incarnation, in our Lord's teaching.

The second thickening or embodiment of the Logos is his presence in creation:

> One could say that the Logos "becomes thick" in the sense that for our sake He ineffably [*aporrētōs*] concealed Himself [*enkrypsas*] in the logoi of beings, and is obliquely signified in proportion to each visible thing, as if through certain letters [*grammatōn*], being whole in whole things while simultaneously remaining utterly complete and fully present, whole, and without diminishment in each particular thing. (*ambig.* 33.2)

Created things are like letters (*grammata*), each with its own logos or internal rational principle, so that each creature obliquely signifies the Logos himself. Just as the ineffable Logos hid himself within Jesus' parables, so he makes himself present in created things by concealing himself (*enkryptein*) in their logoi or internal principles.

Finally, Maximus speaks of the Logos's embodiment within the words of Scripture:

> One could say that the Logos "becomes thick" in the sense that, for the sake of our thick minds, He consented to be both embodied [*sōmatōthēnai*] and expressed through letters, syllables, and utterances [*grammasi kai syllabais kai phōnais*], so that from all these He might gradually gather those who follow Him to Himself, being united by the Spirit, and thus raise us up to the simple and unconditioned idea of Him, bringing us for His own sake into union with Himself by contraction [*systeilas*] to the

---

[11]Similarly, in *ambig.* 10.29, commenting on the transfiguration, Maximus comments that the disciples were taught here that the radiance shining from the Lord's face "was a symbol of His divinity, which transcends intellect, sensation, being, and knowledge," so that from the knowledge of his incarnation, they were led to the glory of his divinity by means of "theological negation [*theologikēs apophaseōs*] that extols Him as being beyond all human comprehension [*achōrēton*]."

same extent that He has for our sake expanded Himself [*diesteilen*] according to the principle of condescension [*synkatabaseōs*]. (*ambig.* 33.2; translation modified)

The simple Logos embodies himself in the letters, syllables, and utterances of Scripture, thereby raising us up to himself.[12] The expansion (*diastellein*) of the Logos in the logoi of Scripture entails, in turn, our contraction (*systellein*) into the Logos. The former is the *exitus* (or *proodos*) from the Logos, the latter, the *reditus* (or *epistrophē*) to the Logos.

The order in which Maximus presents the three thickenings or embodiments may at first seem odd. A chronological order would seem to demand that he move from creation, via Scripture, to Christ. Maximus, however, begins with the Logos's embodiment in Christ; only after that does he speak of creation and of Scripture. The order is undoubtedly theologically motivated. The Confessor was convinced that the incarnation itself is the archetypal embodiment—the original source or *archē*—on which every other speech of God (including creation and Scripture) is patterned. For Maximus, the incarnation "is the blessed end [*telos*] for which all things were brought into existence" (*qu. Thal.* 60.3). If the incarnation functioned, from the outset, as the end or purpose of creation, then theologically, the Christ event precedes the creation of the world, even if chronologically creation precedes the incarnation.

This christological starting point of Maximus's doctrine of creation is best understood against its Irenaean backdrop. For the second-century bishop Irenaeus, too, God's creation of the world had served the larger purpose of incarnation. As he famously wrote: "Inasmuch as the Savior existed beforehand, it was necessary that what was to be saved should also

---

[12]Cf. *ambig.* 10.29, where Maximus states that Christ's dazzling white garments in the transfiguration "convey a symbol: first, of the words of Holy Scripture, which at that moment became bright, clear, and transparent to them, grasped by the intellect without any dark riddles [*griphōdous ainigmatos*] or symbolic shadows [*symbolikou skiasmatos*], and pointing to the meaning [*logos*] that lay concealed [*kalyptomenon*] within them (at which point the disciples received the perfect and correct knowledge of God, and were set free from every attachment to the world and the flesh); and, second, of creation itself—stripped of the soiled preconceptions of those who till then believed they saw it clearly, but who in fact were deceived and bound to sense perception alone—now appearing in the variety of the different forms [*eidōn*] that constitute it, all declaring the power of the Creator Word, in the same way that a garment makes known the dignity of the one who wears it."

exist, so that the Savior would not be something without a purpose" (*haer.* 3.22.3).[13] For Irenaeus, the preexistence of Christ as Savior, and God's intention to become human in Christ, called for the creation of human beings. We could read the passage from Maximus almost as a commentary on the famous line from Irenaeus. For Maximus, too, all things were brought into existence for the sake of the incarnation; all things exist for the sake of the goal of the incarnation. On Maximus's understanding, if the mystery of the incarnation was "foreknown before the foundation of the world," and if it functioned as the end or purpose of creation, then theologically, the incarnation must be the grand, archetypal event.[14]

Not only is the incarnation the original archetypal reality of every embodiment of the Logos, but, as the archetype, Christ also recapitulates all things—Maximus's recapitulation discourse, too, going back to Irenaeus. Christ, suggests Maximus, "is, properly speaking, the limit and goal [*peras*] of God's providence [*pronoias*], and of the things under His providential care [*pronooumenōn*], since the recapitulation [*anakephalaiōsis*] of the things created by God is God Himself" (*qu. Thal.* 60.3). God himself retraces or recapitulates all of creation (cf. Eph 1:10) in and through our incarnate Lord, and by this perfect retracing sums up all things in Christ. Every other embodiment is, therefore, a type of Christ. The embodied logoi of creation and Scripture are typologically patterned upon the archetypal embodiment of the Word made flesh.[15] The incarnation as archetype implies both that it is theologically primary or original and that everything existing typologically relates to him as the one who retraces and so perfects their being.

---

[13]Irenaeus, *St. Irenaeus of Lyons: Against the Heresies*, book 3, ed. Irenaeus M. C. Steenberg, trans. Dominic J. Unger, Ancient Christian Writers 64 (New York: Newman Press, 2012).

[14]Hans Urs von Balthasar comments: "It is very significant that Maximus represents the Incarnation of the Logos and the whole historical course of the world's salvation as both a primeval idea of God and as the underlying structure of his overall plan of the world and that he designates the mystery of the Cross, grave, and Resurrection [of Christ] as the basis and goal of creation." *Cosmic Liturgy: The Universe According to Maximus the Confessor*, trans. Brian E. Daley (San Francisco: Ignatius, 2003), 120; square brackets original. Cf. 133-34.

[15]This priority of the incarnation vis-à-vis the other embodiments of the Logos means, in my view, that according to Maximus, the latter are analogically patterned upon the former. *Pace* Jordan Daniel Wood, *The Whole Mystery of Christ: Creation as Incarnation in Maximus Confessor* (Notre Dame, IN: University of Notre Dame Press, 2023). See Hans Boersma, "God as Embodied: Christology and Participation in Maximus the Confessor," *St Vladimir's Theological Quarterly* 67, nos. 1-2 (2023): 147-69.

For Maximus, then, the incarnation was not an afterthought. The Confessor, says Paul Blowers, "does not allow Christ himself to be treated merely as a *deus ex machina* introduced at the most strategic or climactic moment in this unfolding drama. Rather, the activity of Christ as the Logos and Wisdom of God saturates the drama from beginning to end."[16] And because creation exists always already with a view to Christ, Christ came not just to deal with human sin, but also—and primarily—with a pedagogical purpose: to disciple Adamic existence into maturity or perfection (*teleiotēs*).

The eschaton, therefore, is not simply a return to an earlier paradisal state. Though Maximus works with an *exitus-reditus* (or *proodos-epistrophē*) schema, the return brings about something more glorious than the initial creation.[17] Divinization takes human beings in and through the hypostatic union of Christ into the Logos, where the saints and all that was good in their lives—what Maximus calls their well-being (*eu einai*)—is transfigured and taken up into the glory of the ineffable Logos.

READING WITH HOPE: REST IN THE END

Maximus, then, though a Neoplatonist, deliberately made room for the historical process of education and maturation through the presence of the Logos in Christ, in creation, and in Scripture. According to Maximus, the Logos employs time and space in the service of this pedagogical process of maturation—something that the radical Platonism of the Origenist tradition had been unable to accommodate. The result was a clash between Maximus and the Origenists. The latter drew on aspects of Origen's *On First Principles* to make the point that, prior to their creation, the souls had been united as rational beings (*logikoi*) within a spiritual *henad* and had thus been at rest in the presence of God.[18] It was thought that some of these

---

[16]Paul M. Blowers, *Maximus the Confessor: Jesus Christ and the Transfiguration of the World* (New York: Oxford University Press, 2016), 108.

[17]Cf. Hans Urs von Balthasar's comment that in Maximus, "Alexandrian speculation about the Logos intersects with a simply linear conception of the divine plan. By conceiving of the Logos— as Origen had done—both as the second Person in God and as the locus of the divine ideas, Maximus is led to conceive the world as an unfolding of the unitary divine Idea and so comes close to the idealist notion of an 'economic' return of all things in the world to their Idea in God." *Cosmic Liturgy*, 117.

[18]Cf. Origen, *Princ.* 2.9.1-2.9.2.

rational beings (*logikoi*) had become weary of contemplating God and so were distracted. This experience of "satiety" (*koros*) had led to their "cooling off" (*psychos*), which turned them into souls (*psychai*).[19] The outcome was a lapse from heavenly contemplation to earthly existence.

Origenism, then, saw the plurality and materiality of human beings as the problematic outcome of angels and humans falling away from God. Thomas Cattoi points to Evagrius Ponticus (345–399) as the key monastic figure transmitting such Origenist ideas to John Cassian, and via John Cassian to the West. Cattoi writes: "Within this cosmological narrative, angels, demons and human beings are nothing but rational beings who have forsaken their intimacy with the divine, and whose different stations in the universe reflect the extent to which they have fallen away from their original condition."[20] The Origenist tradition regarded both plurality and materiality as inherently problematic.

The Origenists undergirded their metaphysic through a triad proceeding from rest (*stasis*) or remaining (*monē*), via movement (*kinēsis*), to origination (*genesis*). Torstein Tollefsen summarizes Origenist thinking about this triad as follows: "The Origenist idea is that intellectual beings are originally gathered around God (this is *monē*), but because of surfeit in their contemplation of God they move away from Him and thereby sin (this is *kinēsi*). As a result, the world is created as a pedagogical institution for the redemption of intellectual creatures (this is *genesis*)."[21] Needless to say, the pedagogy that Tollefsen has in mind is a semi-Gnostic form of education that attempts to undo the lapse into the created world, since along with plurality and materiality, the world of time, movement, and bodily existence are all evaluated in strictly negative fashion.[22]

Maximus rearranged the elements of the triad by distinguishing clearly between Creator and creature. He insisted that the Creator is "immovable" (*akinēton*), while everything else—that which has received its

---

[19] Andreas Andreopoulos, "Eschatology in Maximus the Confessor," in *Oxford Handbook of Maximus*, 326-27.

[20] Thomas Cattoi, "Liturgy as Cosmic Transformation," in *Oxford Handbook of Maximus*, 419.

[21] Tollefsen, *Christocentric Cosmology*, 75.

[22] Origenist anthropology was dualistic: neither the initial rest (*stasis*) nor the final return to God involves the body. Cf. Andreopoulos, "Eschatology," 327.

being ex nihilo—is "in motion" (*kinēton*). Created things, therefore, have
not yet come to "rest" (*prosanapausan*) (*ambig.* 7.3). Twice Maximus
speaks of the "ultimate desired end" (*eschaton orekton*), as something
that created things are still moving toward (*ambig.* 7.3). In short, because
God is always at rest (being immovable) whereas creatures still long for
their rest (since they are in motion), "rest" is not the first element of the
triad (as is the case with Origenist *stasis*), but the last.[23]

Essentially, then, Maximus reversed the Origenist triad, replacing the
triad of rest (*stasis*) to movement (*kinēsis*) to origination (*genesis*) with
that of origination (*genesis*) to movement (*kinēsis*) to rest (*stasis*).[24] This
reversal was significant for several reasons. First, it rejected speculation
about satiety (*koros*) of spiritual beings in the divine world. This Origenist
notion tended to equate creation and fall: the very movement away from
rest was viewed as a lapse (fall) into creation. To be sure, in rejecting this
understanding, Maximus did not put aside the idea of creation as coming
from God and as moving back to God. As we have already seen, the underlying schema of his metaphysic was that of *exitus* or expansion (*diastellein*) and of *reditus* or contraction (*systellein*)—a distinctly Neoplatonist
schema. But the significant difference between Maximus and the Origenists is that Maximus regarded the origination of created being as basically good; it is not a lapse from God resulting from boredom.

Maximus maps upon his threefold schema of beginning, movement,
and rest his well-known distinction between being (*einai*), well-being
(*eu einai*), and eternal well-being (*aei eu einai*) (*ambig.* 7.10; cf. 10.12).
Since God is beginning (*archē*) and end (*telos*) (cf. Rev 21:6), we have

---

[23] Cf. the helpful discussion about "rest" in Maximus in Alexis Torrance, *Human Perfection in
Byzantine Theology: Attaining the Fullness of Christ* (New York: Oxford University Press,
2020), 40-81.

[24] Cf. *ambig.* 7.15: "The beginning of every natural motion is the origin (*genesis*) of the things that
are moved, and the beginning of the origin of whatever has been originated is God, for He is
the author of origination. The end of the natural motion of whatever has been originated is rest
[*stasis*], which, after the passage beyond finite things, is produced completely by infinity, for in
the absence of any spatial or temporal interval, every motion of whatever is naturally moved
ceases, henceforth having nowhere, and no means whereby, and nothing to which it could be
moved, since it has attained its goal and cause, which is God, who is Himself the limit of the
infinite horizon that limits all motion. Thus the beginning and end of every origin and motion
of beings is God, for it is from Him that they have come into being, and by Him that they are
moved, and it is in Him that they will achieve rest."

both our beginning and our end in him. From the creaturely perspective, the former is being (*einai*), the latter, eternal well-being (*aei eu einai*), so that the end surpasses the beginning. It is love—Maximus uses the verb *eraō*—that carries us beyond ourselves by way of "ecstasy" (*ekstasin*), so as to be entirely encompassed by our beloved (*ambig.* 7.10).

The Confessor has reworked the Neoplatonist schema of exit and return by highlighting the in-between stage of well-being (*eu einai*). This stage is characterized by the thickening or embodiment of the Logos in Christ, creation, and Scripture. Maximus often speaks of the movement within this stage as an opportunity for learning how to read. He comments, for instance,

> Having granted existence to the entire visible creation, God did not leave it to be moved about solely by means of sense perception, but implanted, within each of the species comprising creation, spiritual principles [*logous*] of wisdom and modes [*tropous*] of graceful conduct. His aim was not only that mute creations should loudly herald Him as their Creator, proclaimed by means of the principles [*logois*] of the things that came into being, but also that the human person, being tutored [*paidagōgoumenon*] by the natural laws and ways of visible realities, should easily find the road of righteousness, which leads to Him. (*qu. Thal.* 51.2)

God, claims Maximus, is a tutor, whose pedagogy leads us to a discernment of the logoi of Christ, creation, and Scripture. It is by discerning the logoi that we are contracted (*systellein*) or enfolded (*complicare*) back into the Logos of God.

For Maximus, then, we come to know Christ through a life of virtue, engage in natural contemplation (*physikē theōria*) of the logoi of creation, and are equipped to read the deeper, spiritual meanings of the divine Scriptures.[25] Together, these reading processes take us to our final rest.

---

[25]Cf. Maximus's comment: "Whoever wishes blamelessly [*amemptōs*] to walk the straight road to God, stands in need of both the inherent spiritual knowledge [*pneumati gnōseōs*] of Scripture, and the natural contemplation [*physikēs theōrias*] of beings according to the spirit. In this way, anyone who desires to become a perfect lover [*teleias erastēn*] of perfect wisdom [*sophias teleion*] will be able to show what is only reasonable, namely, that the two laws—the natural and the written—are of equal value and equal dignity, that both of them reciprocally teach the same things, and that neither is superior or inferior to the other" (*ambig.* 10.30).

The question we face in our personal lives is how we use our freedom (*proairesis*)—whether for good or ill, in line with our final end or not. Or, to put it differently, the question is whether we take the educational opportunity to learn how to read. Reading is inherently a hopeful act because through reading the logoi—of Christ, creation, and Scripture—we reach our eternal well-being.

This pedagogical process depends, for Maximus, upon our mutability. Movement, mutability, and historical progression all received positive valuation in Maximus's schema, as they allow for pedagogical development and growth toward the maturity or perfection of our final rest.[26] As Maximos Constas rightly concludes, the Confessor viewed the final goal no longer simply as a return to the beginning but instead as "an ontologically unprecedented union with God in a final, eschatological, and divinizing consummation."[27] Maximus worked with a biblically derived teleological schema, in which rest serves as the end toward which all creaturely motion tends.[28]

If the Origenists were correct in positing rest or *stasis* as the beginning rather than the end—and if this rest had been shattered by satiety—then, Maximus objects, wouldn't we run the risk of bliss being destroyed all over again in the hereafter? What is preventing this event from recurring? "If what they [i.e., the Origenists] say is true, it necessarily follows that rational beings, when found in the same circumstances, will undergo the same changes *ad infinitum*" (*ambig.* 7.4). And, Maximus adds, if these rational beings had been able but not willing to abide in beauty (*kalon*), then this beauty would not be desirable in and of itself. In fact, beauty and evil (*kakon*) would have a similar

---

[26]Despite Maximus's emphasis on eternal rest, he does speak of the eschaton in several passages as "ever-moving rest" (*aeikinētos stasis*), which betrays the influence of Gregory of Nyssa's notion of "eternal progress" (*epektasis*). See Andreopoulos, "Eschatology," 328. Cf. also Paul M. Blowers, "Maximus the Confessor, Gregory of Nyssa, and the Concept of 'Perpetual Progress,'" *Vigiliae Christianae* 46 (1992): 151-71.

[27]Maximos Constas, "Maximus the Confessor, Gregory of Nyssa, and the Transformation of Christian Neoplatonism," *Analogia* 2 (2017): 9.

[28]Cf. *ambig.* 10.84, where Maximus speaks of the end of all things as "ushering in a condition in which no beings will move [*pheron*] or be moved [*pheromenon*], for there will be no movement [*kinēsis*] at all, but rather an ineffable stillness [*pagiotētos arrētou*] that will contain the flow and motion [*phoran*] of whatever is carried along [*pheromenōn*] and moved [*kinoumenōn*]."

status, since evil would be necessary in order to learn what is good (*ambig.* 7.5).[29]

Maximus unpacks his teleology by appealing both to Aristotle ("a man who was an outsider to the faith") and to Scripture. The Confessor quotes Aristotle as saying, "The end [*telos*] is that for the sake of which all things exist; it, however, is for the sake of nothing."[30] Maximus distinguishes between "that which is perfect in itself" (*autoteles*), which is uncaused, impassible, unique, infinite, and uncircumscribed, and therefore not subject to movement, and that which has not yet arrived at its "ultimate desired end" (*eschatou . . . orektou*). Creatures in this life have not yet arrived at the aim of their desire, and so Maximus concludes that "it cannot be maintained that a movement of rational beings previously at rest in a primordial unity [*henados*] subsequently brought corporeal bodies into being" (*ambig.* 7.7). Aristotle's teleological logic regarding perfect and imperfect being defeats the Origenist schema.

Aristotle is not, however, in the driver's seat for Maximus, as Maximus immediately adds scriptural testimonies that make clear we still await the final end of our perfect rest:[31]

- Genesis 3:22—"Lest he put forth his hand, and take also of the tree of life, and eat, and live for ever."

- Deuteronomy 12:9—"Ye are not as yet come to the rest and to the inheritance, which the LORD your God giveth you."

- Psalm 17:15—"I shall be satisfied, when I awake, with thy likeness."

- Psalm 42:2—"My soul thirsteth for God, for the living God: When shall I come and appear before God?"

- Philippians 3:11–12—"If by any means I might attain unto the resurrection of the dead. Not as though I had already attained, either

---

[29]Cf. *ambig.* 7.29: "We do not conceive of the Good as something so narrowly circumscribed and ignoble, as if it could induce a kind of satiety and provoke a rebellion among those whose desire it could not satisfy."

[30]Maximus refers to Aristotle's *Met.* 2.2, 994b or 3.4, 999b by way of the *Selecta in psalmos* (PG 12.1053A), attributed to Origen. See Nicholas Constas's comment on this in Maximus the Confessor, *On Difficulties*, 479n9.

[31]The biblical quotations are all taken from the King James Version.

were already perfect: but I follow after, if that I may apprehend that for which also I am apprehended of Christ Jesus."

- Hebrews 4:10—"For he that is entered into his rest, he also hath ceased from his own works, as God did from his."
- Hebrews 11:39—"And these all, having obtained a good report through faith, received not the promise."
- Matthew 11:28—"Come unto me, all ye that labour and are heavy laden, and I will give you rest."

Scripture itself, according to Maximus, makes clear that rest pertains to the end rather than to the beginning. Aristotle's telos, therefore, must refer to the God of the Scriptures: he, claims Maximus, is the end, the perfection, and the impassible, because he is unmoved, complete, and dispassionate. By contrast, beings (things that have come to be) "suffer" or "experience" (*paschei*) movement toward God (*ambig.* 7.9).

Maximus's pedagogy of reading—a process that leads to the maturation or perfection of deification—is yet another element of his theology that goes back to Saint Irenaeus. The bishop of Lyons had regarded Adam and Eve as infants, created for maturity in Christ.[32] The entire history of redemption, therefore, was an exercise in divine pedagogy, God training his children by "accustoming [*assuescens*] man to bear His Spirit" (*haer.* 4.14.2).[33] The law, according to Irenaeus, was a gift of God to the Israelites, suited to their servile, immature character, which over time they outgrew in their maturity. Irenaeus distinguished between three stages of the vision of God—prophetic, adoptive, and paternal vision—which God used as a pedagogical method to accustom his people to the increasing immediacy of seeing God (*haer.* 4.20.5).[34] Using Maximian language, we might say that God's gracious "principle of condescension" (*ambig.* 33.2) opened up the possibility of a movement

---

[32] See *haer.* 3.22.4; 4.20.5; 4.38.1-4; *On the Apostolic Preaching*, ed. and trans. John Behr, Popular Patristics 17 (Crestwood, NY: St Vladimir's Seminary Press, 1997), 14-15.

[33] Cf. Hans Boersma, "Justification Within Recapitulation: Irenaeus in Ecumenical Dialogue," *International Journal of Systematic Theology* 22 (2020): 183-84.

[34] Cf. Hans Boersma, *Seeing God: The Beatific Vision in Christian Tradition* (Grand Rapids, MI: Eerdmans, 2018), 401-4.

of well-being (*eu einai*)—that is, a pedagogy of hope in which God's people are increasingly brought toward the maturity of deification itself. In short, for Maximus, reading was an act of hope since it is reading the logoi of divine embodiment in Christ, creation, and Scripture that leads to our deification. Reading or discerning the logoi through free will (*proairesis*) brings us to our proper end (*ambig.* 7.10). This internal power of the will, Maximus claims, sets us on the right path of motion and will continue to characterize us even at the stage of complete deification (*ambig.* 7.12). At that point, by means of a "surrender of will" (*ekchōrēsin gnōmikēn*), our will ends up aligning fully with God's (Mt 26:39; Gal 2:20). This loving motion, therefore, involves the "suffering" (*paschei*) of ecstasy—a gift from the "grace of the Spirit"—that unites our energy with that of God. The result is that we will be entirely deified. That is to say, our motion and activity (*energeia*) will come to rest in that of God. God's pedagogy comes to its intended end, and our activity of reading ceases, since we will have received the deifying energy of God.[35]

Reading is a practice of hope only when it is well done. Maximus reminds us that it is well-being (*eu einai*) that brings us to our divinizing telos. When we read skillfully or virtuously—the one Greek word *aretē* including both aspects—we read not for entertainment or for selfish pleasure; instead, our reading is (1) a discernment of the logoi of divine embodiment and (2) a practice through which we align ourselves with our own individual logos, since God intends to bring us to maturity or perfection in his eternal Logos. Reading, then, is serious business—ascetic business, really—which requires selfless renunciation, deliberate choices, and passionate focus upon the Word as our end. In a nominalist culture, where words are just words, words become cheap; as a result, reading, too, is cheapened.[36] Only within a realist metaphysic such as that

---

[35]Our being "will have become God by divinization." *ambig.* 7.12; cf. 1.91.

[36]To be sure, the cheapening of words is not just the result of a nominalist metaphysic. Augustine already struggled with the cheapening of words: "By being uttered all the time, every day, words have become cheap [*viluerunt*] to us—words just sounding and then ceasing have grown stale; they seem to be nothing more than words. But there is also a word within a human person that abides there, for only the sound comes out of the mouth. There is the word which is really spoken in the spirit, that which you understand from the sound but which is not itself the sound." "Homily 1," in *Homilies on the Gospel of John 1–40*, trans. Edmund Hill, ed. Allan D. Fitzgerald,

of Saint Maximus the Confessor is it possible to retain the hopeful character of reading.

Such a realist metaphysic does not impose an alien (say, Neoplatonist) framework onto a biblical account. Maximus refused to separate philosophy and theology or nature and the supernatural. The embodiment of the Logos in this world is, archetypically, the incarnation of the Logos in Jesus Christ. Only when we take our starting point within this central embodiment of the Logos can we also come to grips with the Logos's embodiments in creation and in Scripture. Jesus Christ, therefore, is the anchor to all hopeful reading. In short, the realist metaphysic of Maximus is deeply Christian because of its overtly christological character.

Finally, reading is hopeful precisely inasmuch as it is not ultimate. Whatever is ultimate is the fulfillment of our hope; in that sense, only God is our hope. Reading is hopeful in a penultimate sense: when done well, it takes us back to God. Logoi are theophanic signs, making present the Logos whom they signify. In the presence of the signified, words fold back into their source and end. Does this mean that our words are finally futile, after all, disappearing in the ocean of the godhead? Far from it. Just as our bodies are raised to eternal life, so too our words have an eternal destiny. Perhaps one way to speak of the eschatological future of the many words we have spoken and read throughout our lives is to say that they, just as our bodies, will be transfigured into glory—in an ineffable (*arrētos*) and unknowable (*agnōstos*) manner joined to the Logos beyond all being and so changed from glory to glory (2 Cor 3:18). Along with all creation, our reading is hopeful because we know that the logoi that we read participate in the Logos—the Word spoken eternally by the Father himself.

SIX

PROPHETS AND POETS AT THE APOCALYPSE

Writing as a Hopeful Educational Practice

JESSICA HOOTEN WILSON

AFTER TEN YEARS OF LIVING IN THE SAME SMALL TOWN, my husband and I undertook to move our whole family across the country, which meant cleaning out an attic. As he patiently carried down each Rubbermaid container from its dusty corner and popped open the lid, we discovered inside too many pages to count of my writing from the ages of six to thirty. My mother had stored away my elementary school poems and high school essay contests and graduate research papers and bequeathed them to us when we married. In these blue and green bins were all the words that had hummed inside of me as a child and played out into verse and sentences over a lifetime. I expected my husband to begrudge these pounds of paper as refuse, but he picked up a few, read lines aloud and responded, "What did I do with my life while you were writing?"

I flipped the question in my head: *What was I doing with my life that I spent so much of it writing?*

When I was eleven, the film *Sister Act 2* came out, and I still re-member when Whoopi Goldberg, who played a singer posing as a nun teaching high school choir—and thus stretching the imaginations of all of us children in the 1990s—quoted (paraphrased) Rainer Maria Rilke: "Don't ask me about being a writer. If when you wake up in the morning, you can think of nothing but writing, then you're a writer." Goldberg repeated this advice to a wayward student, "If you wake up in the morning and you can't think of anything but singing first, then you're supposed to be a singer." I resonated so much with that moment. The actual line from Rilke's *Letters to a Young Poet* is "Must I write? Dig down into yourself for a deep answer. And if this should be in the af-firmative, if you meet this solemn question with a strong and simple 'I must,' then build your life according to this necessity."[1] I have answered yes; I am a writer.

But my husband is not a writer; he is an engineer. Should he write? Should everyone write? I can affirm that I am made to write, and, to that end, I quote *Chariots of Fire* loosely, "I feel God's pleasure in me" when I write. However, is there a theological imperative to write? Is there something within the Christian anthropology that understands human beings as *homo scribens*?

We have no record of Jesus ever writing a word, unless you count that enigmatic scribbling in the dirt at the feet of the adulteress about to be stoned (Jn 8:8). Socrates never wrote a word. Those two ancient examples seem to end any argument about the virtue of writing before it even begins. If human beings are meant to write, why didn't Jesus, the God-man, the most Human One, do so? Why did Socrates, arguably the world's most famous philosopher, petition against writing as a new-fangled technology that harbored grim consequences for humanity?

Writing begins at least as early in human history as 3500 BC.[2] We have poetry, history, laws—all written down in the ancient world. Yet in 370 BC, Socrates decries writing as a practice that will detract from the human soul:

---

[1] Rainer Maria Rilke, *Letters to a Young Poet,* trans. Reginald Snell (Mineola, NY: Dover, 2012), 12.
[2] The Kish tablet. See Steven Roger Fischer, *A History of Writing,* rev. ed. (London: Reaktion, 2020).

If men learn this [writing], it will implant forgetfulness in their souls; they will cease to exercise memory because they rely on that which is written, calling things to remembrance no longer from within themselves, but by means of external marks. What you have discovered is a recipe not for memory, but for reminder. And it is no true wisdom that you offer your disciples, but only its semblance, for by telling them of many things without teaching them you will make them seem to know much, while for the most part they know nothing, and as men filled, not with wisdom but with the conceit of wisdom, they will be a burden to their fellows.[3]

Although we could debate Socrates about the good of writing—which is, ironically, the subject of this chapter—he is not wrong that human beings have lost the capability of remembering once practiced by the ancients. We rely on the written word and even more now on Google. Yet it is also true that we would not be able to discuss Socrates's wisdom had Plato not written it down.

In the Judeo-Christian Scriptures, God commands several of his people to write. While Jerusalem awaits destruction by Babylon, the prophet Habakkuk calls to God in distress, and the Lord answers not with salvation but with the charge to write: "Then the LORD replied: 'Write down the revelation / and make it plain on tablets / so that a herald may run with it'" (Hab 2:2 NIV). The Lord does the same thing to Habakkuk's contemporary Jeremiah: "Write in a book all the words I have spoken to you" (Jer 30:2 NIV).

The Pentateuch is author-credited to Moses, whom God instructs several times in Exodus to write down everything from the Ten Commandments to Israel's itinerary from Egypt to the promised land (Ex 17:14; 34:27). All the way from Moses to Saint John in Revelation, where the apostle hears, "Write, therefore what you have seen" (Rev 1:19 NIV), God seems intent on his people writing.

So if theological imperatives to write exist, we must ask, "Why?" In "Why I Write," the British novelist George Orwell proposes at least four reasons: sheer egoism; aesthetic enthusiasm; historical impulse; or political

---

[3]Plato, *Phaedrus*, trans. R(eginald) Hackforth (Cambridge: Cambridge University Press, 1952), 274c-275b.

purpose.[4] Setting aside writing out of ego, which does not align with Christian character, the other three possibilities correlate well with what we find in the Scriptures. There are at least three genres that God directs his people to write: history; prophecy; and poetry.[5] All these genres exhibit writing as a hopeful practice—not only for the reader in the message of the texts, which is true, but also for the writer in the process demanded by the activity. The Bible becomes a model for what writing as a spiritual practice should look like. The Bible writers' explorations of history, prophecy, and poetry illuminate for us how writing is much more than an amateur hobby; it is a virtuous discipline, one that teaches us hope.

History and Writing as Hopeful

The history Moses records in Genesis through Deuteronomy does not, on the surface, appear hopeful. The stories exhibit a litany of human failure. But the providence of God is on display in this history. In defiance of Socrates's concern that writing will erase memory, the Lord requires Moses to write down their history so that the people remember it: "Only take care, and keep your soul diligently, lest you forget the things that your eyes have seen, and lest they depart from your heart all the days of your life. Make them known to your children and your children's children" (Deut 4:9 ESV). By remembering their history, the Israelites will be able to hope in God's promises to them. Their hope lies not in who they are—that way lies disaster—but in who God is. The call to write their history provides the opportunity to practice hope.

In 1967, Catholic philosopher Josef Pieper tied hope and history together in five lectures delivered in Salzburg titled *Hope and History*. Pieper distinguishes between the ephemeral things for which we hope and the singular hope only to be fulfilled after history. "How do things stand regarding our hope if we nevertheless must die?" Pieper asks.[6] Pieper explores the relationship between hope and history not abstractly

---

[4]George Orwell, "Why I Write," *Gangrel* 4 (Summer 1946), Orwell Foundation, www.orwellfoundation .com/the-orwell-foundation/orwell/essays-and-other-works/why-i-write/.

[5]God also decrees that laws be written down, a genre we will not consider.

[6]Josef Pieper, *Hope and History*, trans. Richard and Clara Winston (Providence, RI: Cluny Media, 2020), 86.

but with vulnerability; he dedicated the book to his son Thomas, who had recently died of a cerebral hemorrhage at age twenty-eight. All of us are on our way, our individual histories being written into the cosmic history. Pieper observes, "The point of time at which the true result of life is revealed continues to lie in the future for exactly as long as that life lasts. At no moment of existence, not even on the threshold of death, can man say: Now I am no longer on my way; fulfillment no longer lies ahead of me."[7] As wayfarers, we must practice the virtue of hope, for we are always living history and awaiting future.

Writing history is a hopeful practice because we both remember the good from the past and also choose not to forget the evil. When Pieper tries to define hope, he notes the obvious: "We speak of hope only when what we expect is *good* for us. . . . Desire, longing, craving, wishes, hunger and thirst must be involved; otherwise we are not talking about hope."[8] It may seem that writing history of past atrocities would not gel with expectations for the good. But the reality of desire or longing is that you *want*—you are lacking something.

The apostle Paul writes, "But hope that is seen is no hope at all. Who hopes for what they already have?" (Rom 8:24 NIV). By remembering the crimes of history, we experience the lack, which instills the hunger for the good in us. Elie Wiesel writes of his time in the concentration camps to not forget the reality of suffering: "Never shall I forget that night, the first night in camp, that turned my life into one long night seven times sealed. Never shall I forget . . . those things, even were I condemned to live as long as God Himself. Never."[9] Writing the horrors of Wiesel's experience has shown readers what to hope for in the future. It also has allowed others to see themselves in this history, and thus hope for a future community.

For Christians, while Genesis narrates the lives of the patriarchs, it is in Exodus that Israel becomes a nation, as Leon Kass argued. In *Founding God's Nation: Reading Exodus*, Kass confesses in the introduction how he learned of his own longings when studying this book of the Bible:

---

[7]Pieper, *Hope and History*, 16.
[8]Pieper, *Hope and History*, 7.
[9]Elie Wiesel, *Night*, trans. Marion Wiesel (New York: Hill & Wang, 2006), 34.

Exodus surely illuminates the process of people formation. . . . It surely offers wise guidance for communal life. . . . But it also examines and nourishes deep longings of the soul for which law and politics are insufficient, longings that I was not fully aware I harbored when I first began this study.[10]

In the process of writing about the history of the Jewish people, Kass learned of a longing within him for a community he had not known, and a transcendent one at that. The writing process created a need for something for which Kass had not previously understood to hope.

At President Bill Clinton's second inauguration, poet Miller Williams read "Of History and Hope," in which he asks, "But where are we going to be, and why, and who?" Although referring to the American people, Williams points to a reality that shared history forms a community. Our "stories" and "old songs" reveal our communal journey from the past into the future. "The children. The children," the poet repeats enigmatically:

All this in the hands of the children, eyes already set
on a land we can never visit—it isn't there yet—
but looking through their eyes, we can see
what our long gift to them may come to be.
If we can truly remember, they will not forget.[11]

Williams highlights how remembering our history teaches the next generation to do likewise. Hope then extends beyond the personal to the communal, beyond the life of one to the lives of many, beyond this generation to the next, and so on.

The reason I decided not to discard all the pages of my past diaries is for the sake of my children; I wanted them to see who I was through the history I had lived—and thereby see the faithfulness of our God—that they too may experience hope.

Prophetic Writing

When we read history recorded in Scripture, we see much of it as exceeding its literal or historical meaning and showcasing a prophetic

---

[10]Leon Kass, *Founding God's Nation: Reading Exodus* (New Haven, CT: Yale University Press 2021), xiii.
[11]"Of History and Hope," Miller Williams, in *Some Jazz a While* (University of Illinois Press, 1999).

meaning. Prophecy includes more than predictions; it offers a subversive way of imagining the past, present, and future. In 1978, the Protestant theologian Walter Brueggemann unpacked the significance of the prophetic imagination as found in the writings of Moses, the prophets, and of course Jesus. His thesis: "The task of prophetic ministry is to nurture, nourish, and evoke a consciousness and perception alternative to the consciousness and perception of the dominant culture around us."[12] Through Brueggemann's explication of the Scriptures, he opens up prophetic writing to all believers, who can imitate this way of seeing and acting in the world. Prophetic writing is hopeful writing because it draws up from beneath the surface things hoped for but unseen.

The commands to write are delivered to the prophets because they are the Lord's dissidents in the world, writing not only about the way things are, but also how they *should* be. In Orwell's conception of why he writes, this is called "political purpose" born from the "desire to push the world in a certain direction, to alter other people's idea of the kind of society that they should strive after."[13] For Christians, this political writing does not stem from personal designs or society's version of utopia but from God's revelation. Pieper, for example, notes how theology transfers historical writing "into a realm of supra-empirical reality" in which history fits "into a more comprehensive universal context which is the proper place of such concepts as 'eternity,' 'kingdom' and 'last judgment.'"[14] Prophetic writing expresses the hope that the promises of revelation are worth moving toward.

Much of today's prophetic writing is found in fiction. Brueggemann notes in passing, "It is precisely the daring work of fiction to probe beyond settled truth and to walk to the edge of alternatives not yet available to us."[15] In her explication of what makes a Catholic novelist, Flannery O'Connor states all fiction writers should be characterized by "prophetic vision," which she clarifies is not about predicting the future: "The prophet is a realist of distances. . . . It is the realism which does not

---

[12]Walter Brueggemann, *The Prophetic Imagination* (Philadelphia: Fortress, 1978), 3.
[13]Orwell, "Why I Write."
[14]Pieper, *Hope and History*, 30.
[15]Walter Brueggemann, *Finally Comes the Poet: Daring Speech for Proclamation* (Philadelphia: Fortress, 1989), 5.

hesitate to distort appearances in order to show a hidden truth."[16] It may be difficult to draw the connecting dots between the prophecy of Ezekiel and the stories of Flannery O'Connor. Yet their writing subverts what Brueggemann calls "the royal consciousness"—in other terms, the worldly perspective or the view of the empire.

To offer one example of prophetic writing, consider O'Connor's 1953 story "A Late Encounter with the Enemy," in which the 104-year-old General Sash is meant to sit on stage for his 62-year-old daughter Sally's college graduation. In her pride, Sally wants to show him off. She prays he'll live until she graduates and imagines holding "her head very high as if she were saying, 'See him! . . . Glorious upright old man standing for the old traditions! Dignity! Honor! Courage!'"[17] But her dream is popped by the old man appearing suddenly behind her naked in his wheelchair, naught but his general's hat on.

The "general" himself is a fake, having been given his costume by the *Gone with the Wind* producers when they premiered the film in Atlanta and lined up former Confederates by the red carpet like props. In this story, O'Connor is overturning the symbols of White supremacy that infected her Southern home. While the defeated Confederates may imagine they were once aristocrats with noble virtues, O'Connor shows that the emperor—or the general, in this case—has no clothes on.

The story concludes with death coming to take General Sash away. A black procession is upon him—both literally, the graduates in their robes, and figuratively, the fingers of death. "He recognized it," the narrator observes, "for it had been dogging all his days. He made such a desperate effort to see over it and find out what comes after the past that his hand clenched the sword until the blade touched bone."[18] O'Connor pushes her reader to consider the relationship between past, present, and future in this moment with an allusion to Hebrews 4:12, "For the word of God is alive and active. Sharper than any double-edged sword, it penetrates even

---

[16]Flannery O'Connor, *Mystery and Manners*, ed. Robert Fitzgerald (New York: Farrar, Straus & Giroux, 1969), 179.
[17]Flannery O'Connor, "A Late Encounter with the Enemy," in *Flannery O'Connor: The Complete Stories* (New York: Farrar, Straus & Giroux, 1971), 135.
[18]O'Connor, "Late Encounter," 143.

to dividing soul and spirit, joints and marrow; it judges the thoughts and attitudes of the heart" (NIV). The general can pretend to be a hero and sit proudly on the stage, an idol for himself, his daughter, and the rest of those attending graduation, but death strips away pretense. The prophetic vision, given by immersion in the Scriptures, sees beneath the surface to what is eternal.

In this way, prophetic writing instructs both writers and readers in hope. "The prophet is one who, by use of these tools of hope," Brueggemann writes—and here the tools are alternative words, images, and symbols—"contradicts the presumed world of kings, showing both that the presumed world does not square with the facts and that we have been taught a lie and have believed it."[19] If writers try to appease the empire, they will only produce propaganda, which leads to despair. But the prophets write against the imperial lies toward a greater hope.

One only has to compare *Gone with the Wind* with O'Connor's "A Late Encounter with the Enemy" to see the difference between propaganda and prophetic writing. With their alternative imagination, the prophets disrupt the pervasive despair. "Thus every totalitarian regime is frightened of the artist," Brueggemann claims, for the artist, as prophet, proposes "futures alternative to the single one the king wants to urge as the only thinkable one."[20]

POETRY OF THE MARTYRS

The prophets speak in images because we cannot write with certainty of what we cannot see here and now, which leads us to our third genre, poetry. Writing of Scripture, Brueggemann asserts,

> When the text comes to speak about this alternative life wrought by God, the text must use poetry. There is no other way to speak. We know about that future—we know surely—but we do not know concretely enough to issue memos and blueprints. We know only enough to sing songs and speak poems. That, however, is enough. We stake our lives on such poems.[21]

---

[19]Brueggemann, *Prophetic Imagination*, 64.
[20]Brueggemann, *Prophetic Imagination*, xx.
[21]Brueggemann, *Finally Comes the Poet*, 41.

Poetic writing names the ineffable, giving voice to the longing that we feel but cannot describe explicitly.

Totalitarian states censor these writers because poems encourage people to desire more than bread and circuses. Through poetic writing, people express a longing for the transcendent. This desire induces a hope that leads readers into action. In *Theology of Hope*, Jürgen Moltmann, for example, explains:

> That is why faith, wherever it develops into hope, causes not rest but unrest, not patience but impatience. It does not calm the unquiet heart, but is itself this unquiet heart in man. Those who hope in Christ can no longer put up with reality as it is, but begin to suffer under it, to contradict it. Peace with God means conflict with the world, for the goad of the promised future stabs inexorably into the flesh of every unfulfilled present.[22]

Poets, in essence, embolden hope.

In her memoir *Hope Against Hope*, Nadezhda Mandelstam (whose name means "hope") writes about the unjust arrest, exile, and eventual death of her husband, the poet Osip Mandelstam, and those like him under the Communist takeover of Russia. She describes him as a man who "couldn't stop telling jokes" and who wrote poetry as though under a compulsion from outside of himself.[23] Speaking of other poets similarly tortured, Nadezhda reflects:

> Banished, sick, penniless and hounded, they still would not give up their power. M. [Osip] behaved like a man conscious of his power and this only egged on those who wanted to destroy him. For them power was expressed in guns, agencies of repression, the distribution of everything— including fame—by coupons. . . . But M. stubbornly maintained that if they killed people for poetry, then they must fear and respect it—in other words, that it too was a power in the land.[24]

Writing poetry paradoxically both removed the poets' worldly power in the USSR and accorded them a power to go on; it granted them hope.

---

[22]Jürgen Moltmann, *Theology of Hope* (New York: Bantam Books, 1966), 449-50.
[23]Nadezhda Mandelstam, *Hope Against Hope* (New York: Random House, 1999), 38.
[24]Mandelstam, *Hope Against Hope*, 170.

Poets continued writing even when confined to gulags, in concentration camps, in prison, or on their deathbeds. Plato notes that Socrates composed verses based on Aesop's fables on the final day of his life prior to his execution by hemlock.[25] Boethius wrote poetry and then philosophy from his cell, locked away and eventually executed by Theodoric in AD 524. The twentieth-century theologian who was executed by the Nazis, Dietrich Bonhoeffer, wrote poetry in his final days.[26]

This unexplainable human impulse continued under Soviet rule. Aleksander Solzhenitsyn would save his bread from his ration to compose poetry as prayer beads, a memory device.[27] Anna Akhmatova would write her verses on paper and ask others to commit them to memory before she burned the evidence.[28] Human beings write poetry because its underlying orientation is a hopeful practice, a practice that defies empires and enkindles souls.

These poets who write even from their places of despair are witnesses to how much writing is a practice of hope. Prior to writing *Hope and History*, Pieper delivered a lecture on the hope of martyrs:

> There was no point in speaking seriously about hope unless there is hope for the martyr, that is, for one whose expectations within this world, whose very prospect of simple survival in the struggle for the realization of justice, have been entirely erased and who therefore, to the superficial view, finds himself in an absolutely desperate situation: in the death cell, the concentration camp, stripped of rights, rendered ridiculous, left alone, exposed to the contempt of the privileged.[29]

Pieper observes that hope is meaningless without considering the witness of martyrs. In some ways, that phrase is redundant, for *witness* is the English equivalent of "martyr" from the Greek.

---

[25] Plato, *Phaedo: The Last Hours of Socrates*, trans. Benjamin Jowett (1892). Available from Project Gutenberg, https://www.gutenberg.org/files/1658/1658-h/1658-h.htm.
[26] Devin Maddox and Taylor Worley, "The Cost of Creativity," *Christianity Today Online,* September 11, 2023, www.christianitytoday.com/ct/2023/october/cost-of-creativity-bonhoeffer-set-aside-ethics-for-art-did.html.
[27] Michael T. Kaufman, "Solzhenitsyn, Literary Giant Who Defied Soviets, Dies at 89," *New York Times*, August 4, 2008, https://www.nytimes.com/2008/08/04/books/04solzhenitsyn.html.
[28] Amanda Haight, *Anna Akhmatova: A Poetic Pilgrimage* (New York: Oxford University Press, 1976), 99.
[29] Pieper, *Hope and History*, 21.

Carolyn Forché coined the term "poetry of witness" after seeing firsthand the human rights abuses during the civil war in El Salvador in 1980. The phrase is not meant to be reduced to political poetry, but in her own words, "In the poetry of witness, the poem makes present to us the experience of the other, the poem *is* the experience, rather than a symbolic representation."[30] Perhaps unintentionally resurrecting the Catholic faith of her upbringing, Forché's language is eucharistic. The poetry of witness is an embodying of words, marked by hope that the martyrs' sufferings will not die with them. Through their writing, these martyrs exhibit an eternal hope that acts as an invitation. "Witness begets witness," Forché writes. "The text we read becomes a living archive." The writing is revived with each new reader. The past is not forgotten. Thus, the future becomes more hopeful.

Apocalypse: The Challenge of AI

Writing is always a futuristic activity, for only the author has access to the immediate present of the composition. In many ways, the writing itself is an act of hope—a reader will exist, words will make sense, and what is concealed within the interior life of the person will be revealed in the words on the page. Flannery O'Connor famously said, "I write because I don't know what I think until I read what I say."[31] Writing is like a mental trust fall—you start putting the pen to paper in the hopes that your words will mean what you think, or that you will discover what you think as you write the words. "When the artist sets about translating his conception into a physical work of stone, or even of verse," explains Pieper, "and when he says he hopes he will succeed, he expresses quite accurately the idea that this success does not depend on himself alone."[32] The writer must hope the words become something more than strings of letters. With each

---

[30] Carolyn Forché, "Reviving the Living Archives: The Witness of Literary Art," in *Poetry of Witness*, ed. Carolyn Forché and Duncan Wu (New York: W.W. Norton, 2014), 26.

[31] This is a quotation often attributed to O'Connor. It seems to be slightly paraphrased from a letter to her agent: "I have to write to discover what I am doing. Like the old lady, I don't know so well what I think until I see what I say; then I have to say it over again." (The "old lady" might be an allusion to an earlier author or literary character.) Flannery O'Connor, *The Habit of Being: Letters of Flannery O'Connor*, ed. Sally Fitzgerald (New York: Vintage Books, 1980), 5.

[32] Pieper, *Hope and History*, 10.

curl of a *q* and cross of an *x*, the writer is bringing something into being, hoping toward the thing the writer envisions but cannot yet see.

William Faulkner insisted writers continued writing because they always failed to complete what they started. "My feeling is that we all fail, that none of it is as good as we all wanted it to be. None of my stuff is as good as I wanted it to be," Faulkner admitted. "That's why I keep on writing another one."[33] What Faulkner does not explicitly point out is the hope required to continue writing. Although he may enjoy what he called "the splendor of failure," without hope that someday his writing might achieve its aim, Faulkner would despair. No writing can be done in actual despair— misery, yes; suffering, yes; but despair, no. Hope is prerequisite for writing.

However, recent technological innovations have challenged our capacity for practicing hope through writing. Chat Generative Pre-trained Transformer (ChatGPT) came out in 2022, enabling consumers to create a written product without the trials of writing. Recently, a pastor confessed to me he employed ChatGPT whenever sermon writing got tough. I recited Romans 5:3-4 in my head, "We know that suffering produces perseverance; perseverance, character; and character, hope" (NIV). How can one learn hope if that person overcomes the inconvenience of sermon writing with the aid of ChatGPT? What will happen to human character? If we hand over the act of writing to the computer, we are losing the opportunity to practice hope.

In 1954, the British children's author Roald Dahl composed his humorous story "The Great Automatic Grammatizator," a precursor in science fiction of today's ChatGPT.[34] The main character, an odd-looking chap named Adolph Knipe, wants to be a writer. After engineering a super-calculator for his employer, Knipe receives a well-deserved holiday. Readers observe him returning to his lonely typewriter where his story "A Narrow Escape" begins, "The night was dark and stormy . . . the rain poured down like cats and dogs." Frustrated by his clichéd attempts at writing, Knipe begins cursing everything around him, until an idea strikes

---

[33]Virginia Colleges Conference, tape 2 from University of Virginia audio recording, April 15, 1957.
[34]See Roald Dahl, *The Great Automatic Grammatizator and Other Stories* (London: Puffin Books, 2001).

him like lightning (see what I did there?). What if he created a machine to write stories for him in the same way that a calculator does math for us?

It's a preposterous idea that a machine could write in place of a human, but soon even his employer is reconciled to it "as a commercial proposition." The machine will "produce the right stuff, at the right time, whenever we want it" in the same way that machines produce "carpets . . . chairs . . . shoes . . . bricks . . . crockery." While Knipe recognizes these machine-made products are inferior, he dismisses that fact as irrelevant. For Knipe—and for the magazines to which he sells his computer-generated stories and for the readers who gobble them up—what matters is the object being generated quickly and efficiently. In the twenty-first century, human beings can actually use "The Great Automatic Grammatizator" in the form of ChatGPT, but what has been lost?

Josef Pieper wrote *Hope and History* following the tragedy of the atomic bomb, but his concerns are relevant analogously to our current situation regarding artificial intelligence (AI). In the introductory chapter to his book, Pieper argues with Immanuel Kant, who thought "the self-destruction of the human species cannot even be considered by a realistic historical thinker; such a thing can never happen." Kant is wrong, Pieper laments, for Hiroshima presents radical evidence to the contrary. "Since then [after the atomic bomb] the idea that mankind might annihilate itself is not only merely conceivable, no longer something arguable; it has become acute."[35] As I am writing this chapter, Russia has invaded Ukraine and Hamas is slaughtering Israeli citizens. I have nightmares about nuclear war as often as 1950s American students dove under desks for bomb drills.

Yet I would gingerly suggest the greatest threat to civilization is not to our physical lives but to our souls. Sooner than a nuclear holocaust, we may bring about a posthuman apocalypse. To this end, Pieper writes, "We are being told, then, that present-day man can hope to be saved from the suicidal situation of the atomic age not by any action of his own, but solely by a genetic change in his physical constitution which may come about in the course of further evolution—a chance which perhaps will

---

[35]Pieper, *Hope and History*, 2.

make him into a different being!"[36] Although Pieper is appalled by this conjecture in the mid-twentieth century, theory is being translated into practice today by tech-entrepreneurs.

For human progress to continue, the next step, for the transhumanists (and now there are even posthumanists), calls for humans to merge with their machines. Instead of embodied souls, we are seen to be half computers and half animals. If only we could enhance the computer side of the human being and decrease the animal nature, then we could will human evolution toward its next advancement.

Although most people who engage with AI do not philosophize its significance, they are ceding their humanity to its mastery unwittingly. It might sound extreme to say ChatGPT dehumanizes the user. However, consider that the goal of ChatGPT is to spit out a product and remove the writer from the process. When we know writing as a process is a human activity by which we practice hope, what then does the human become when the human substitutes the made thing for the journey of making?

Writing is a process, but too often we forget the process and focus on the product. Human beings are in-process creatures: we begin as fetuses, then our flesh and souls journey into maturity. Even after death, we venture on to be transfigured in eternity. Just as we are never finished, neither are our works complete. Throughout life, in imitation of our Creator, we create: books, homes, symphonies. Yet all of these made things are still unfinished, not quite what we hoped they'd be, awaiting heavenly completion. As Karl Rahner observes, "In the torment of the insufficiency of everything attainable, we learn that ultimately in this world there is no finished symphony."[37] We are on our way, and hope is the virtue needed for wayfarers. By emphasizing the immanent product rather than the journey, we extract the virtue of hope from the writing act.

Ideas for Teaching Writing as a Hopeful Activity

Assign a variety of genres of writing: commonplace books, diary entries, poetry, literary criticism, speeches, sermons, and so on. Many teachers

---

[36]Pieper, *Hope and History*, 44.
[37]Karl Rahner, *Servants of the Lord* (New York: Herder & Herder, 1968), 152.

designate these tasks of writing online in discussion boards and so forth, which is fine, as it goes. If you want to be countercultural, try requiring students to use a paper commonplace book, where they are forced to write with pens and practice analog activity rather than writing mediated by a screen. Teach students to value the paper, the pen, the hard copies of the written books, the interaction with the pages of a writer, and the feeling of accomplishment when they keep the journal in their own hand after a class rather than forget what was typed on a screen.

Rather than grading or heavily marking only the final product, emphasize the process with regular input on drafts and/or oral and written feedback. I offer students multiple attempts to submit their work, and I refuse to put a letter or a number on a draft. The goal is to set their eyes on writing as a process; with this in mind, I do not undermine that agenda by focusing on the submitted product. They can revise and rewrite as many times as they desire before the end of the term, and only then will I put forth a grade (as required by our educational system).

Ask for written reflections on the writing process. After students have written something, have them consider its strengths, weaknesses, places where they learned something they did not know before. You could pose the following or similar questions: What did you enjoy about the writing process? Where do you wish you could have spent more time? What thoughts or pieces of evidence challenged you to wrestle with the wording? And so on. Again, I usually ask for these reflections to be written with pen and paper, but they can also be oral discussion.

Read writers on writing. Reading books on writing should not be an activity only for writers; after all, I read books on the periodic table, and I'm not a scientist. We are all human beings who should engage what it means to be creatures of the book, people made by words. C. S. Lewis wrote one of my favorites for this topic: *On Writing (and Writers): A Miscellany of Advice and Opinions.* For a grammar guide that is personal and funny, I recommend *Dreyer's English* by Benjamin Dreyer. But there are many more books on writing that are worth engaging, including those by Annie Dillard, Julia Cameron, Alice Walker, Stephen King, and others.

Read Scripture in writing classes. Christian universities should encourage reading Scripture in writing classes, showing from the Bible examples for why we should write. I began this chapter with several Scripture verses that mention writing. When I was a student at a Christian university, my Bible classes were kept rather separate from my creative writing classes. What would it look like to get out of our academic silos and relate to one another's disciplines—especially when it concerns the relationship between the Word and the words we are putting together?

Alice Walker conjectures that the point of writing is healing: "I think writing really helps you heal yourself. I think if you write long enough, you will be a healthy person." As with other agnostics or pagans, Walker is so close to the truth. However, she places the wrong subject in charge of the verb. She taps into the reality that writing seems to heal our brokenness, as all spiritual practices are apt to do. In this fallen world, we are fractured. Augustine points out how we are disintegrated selves. Howard Thurman indicates the ways our sickness has led to hate toward others and fragmented community. We could come up with a host of witnesses that observe the general truth that "we are unknown to ourselves, we knowers," and to others (to quote Friedrich Nietzsche). By writing, we begin to know our own thoughts again—to see them before us in wholeness rather than in disarray. We expect readers to read them, and thus we invite hospitality to overcome distance. Writing is the healing balm as described by Walker because of how writing reunites the wrecked self with other wrecked selves.

In a world plagued by loneliness, filled with anxiety and mental health crises, where suicide is a leading cause of death, what could be more hopeful than an activity that heals? We have missed out on the way of treating our illness by making writing an academic activity or solely an intellectual or emotional one. In reality, writing is a spiritual practice because it fuses again our heads, hearts, and bodies into a common activity. And it does so with the great hope that someone—maybe only our future self?—will read the words we have written. We write with anticipation, in faith that the future will happen, and with hope that what we do in the present matters. Through writing, we join the prophets, poets, and witnesses of the past, and say, "Come, see what I have seen." And then, "Tell me, what do you see?"

SEVEN

"ARDUOUS AND DIFFICULT TO OBTAIN"

Teaching as a Hopeful Educational Practice

DAVID I. SMITH

AS I PREPARED TO WRITE THIS CHAPTER, I was haunted by a line from one of Walter Brueggemann's eloquent prayers, a prayer of longing for the coming of God's kingdom amid our experience of violence and suffering. "We are people grown weary of waiting," Brueggemann writes. "We dwell in the midst of cynical people, and we have settled for what we can control."[1] Here is one way of articulating the failure of hope: settling for what we can control.

Control is, of course, not a bad thing in itself. I take Brueggemann here to be questioning the kind of control that seeks to close the horizon of possibility so that life, and the people with whom we share it, can be manipulated for our convenience. Such control suggests presumption, yet, as Brueggemann suggests, it can arise from a kind of giving up, a surrender of riskier hopes in favor of manageable routines.

---

[1]Walter Brueggemann, *Awed to Heaven, Rooted in Earth: Prayers of Walter Brueggemann* (Minneapolis: Fortress, 2003), 149.

I offer three examples to illustrate how such a descent might inhabit teaching.

The first is a moment many years ago, when I was teaching French and German at an urban secondary school in England. Social and economic needs among the school population were high, reading levels were low, student capacity for sitting still in classrooms was modest. I was also working for a Christian nonprofit on a curriculum project. One day, during a rare moment of respite, I sat in the resource room with my department chair and explained what I was trying to change in my teaching.

I was struck by the consumerist bent of the standard course materials. Young language learners were asked to spend much of their time talking about eating and shopping, hobbies and travel, cinemas and restaurants. The scenarios they were expected to rehearse typically implied a level of affluence that was beyond the experience of many of my current students. As we laboriously chipped away at the language skills needed for asking foreigners for things while traveling, our efforts were punctuated by the defensible protest that "I am never going to go to France."

The curriculum project in which I was involved focused on ways of fostering moral and spiritual development across the school curriculum.[2] French and German were part of the school curriculum, so I was spending a great deal of time wondering what moral and spiritual development would look like in a language classroom. Our writing team developed a range of approaches including teaching units that invited learners to explore the life story of an elderly refugee, examine the motives of a student resistance group in Nazi Germany, listen to teenagers from Burkina Faso discussing their views on truth telling, and more.[3] The team approached language skills with the hope that more than language could be learned, that at the same time as gaining academically and linguistically, students might listen to strangers, reflect on interpersonal ethics, or consider the possibility of sacrifice for a just cause.

---

[2]See John Shortt, "The Rationale of the Charis Project," in *Spiritual and Religious Education*, ed. Mal Leicester, Celia Modgill, and Sohan Modgill (London: Falmer, 2000), 160-70.

[3]See, e.g., David I. Smith, "Teaching (and Learning from) the White Rose," in *Critical Essays on Resistance in Education*, ed. David M. Moss and Terry A. Osborn, Counterpoints: Studies in the Postmodern Theory of Education (New York: Peter Lang, 2010), 67-82.

Now I sat in the resource room with my department chair and showed her drafts of the new materials. I explained the stories and said a little about the successes and challenges of my first experiments with my students. After listening for some time, she sat back and declared the material was much better than what she was doing in her classroom—more meaningful, more compelling, more educational. She also rejected the idea of ever being able to use it herself. It was enough of a challenge to get the students to comply with learning, she explained. If she came to class with something that really mattered to her, and the students still rejected it, she would be devastated. The risk felt too great. Better to settle for a degree of control.

A second example caught my attention more recently, when my wife asked for a Spanish grammar book for Christmas. When it arrived, I began reading the introduction. The opening sentences are as follows: "Grammar is one of the most difficult (read: boring!) parts of learning a language. Unfortunately, it's something that cannot be left on the sidelines or learned as an afterthought."[4] Two sentences into the text we are told that the topic is difficult, that difficult is equivalent to boring, and that all of humanity finds grammar to be devoid of interest, but it's sadly necessary to learn it.

This opening gambit may be reaching for empathy, an attempt to articulate concern for less motivated learners and an admission that not everything teachers find fascinating will automatically thrill their students. Yet I think it achieves cynicism. I know you don't want to learn and the material is inherently tedious, it says, but I still have to teach. Perhaps if I position myself alongside you in your disaffection, I can at least buy some solidarity. Let's settle for getting through this.

My third example is quite recent. A few months ago, I provided professional development for faculty from various disciplines at a Christian university. I presented some of the things that I will discuss later in this chapter, talking about ways to design teaching and learning processes that meet academic goals but also aspire to something more. One example focused on building a mutually accountable community during a course, creating concrete ways for students to care for one another while

---

[4]Frédéric Bibard, *Spanish Grammar for Beginners: The Most Complete Textbook and Workbook for Beginners* (San Bernardino, CA: My Daily Spanish [https://MyDailySpanish.com], 2019), v.

also enhancing one another's learning. An attendee later described to me a colleague's protest that their course was already so full that they could not possibly make room for accountability in small groups. The social and logistical pressures on teaching are all too real. One convenient response is to settle for content coverage.

These are relatively mild failures of virtue. I chose them precisely because they are ordinary moments, not dramatic collapses. They are routine capitulations to the stresses of the teaching environment. Avoiding such capitulations is not easy. As Brueggemann's prayer says,

> We are people grown weary of waiting.
> We dwell in the midst of cynical people,
>   and we have settled for what we can control.

There are many factors in teaching that the teacher cannot control. We cannot control the context in which schooling happens or the ways that context impinges upon our work. The pandemic and the stresses of tribalized political discourses that often have schools in their crosshairs added to the pressures of an already difficult job. We often cannot control the processes by which larger institutions of which we are part make teaching feel less authentic, less rewarding, more bureaucratic. We cannot control the range of emotional and behavioral responses that students bring to our classrooms.

In an article titled "Love and Despair in Teaching," Daniel Liston draws upon a short story by Andre Dubus to evoke the peculiar despair that can arise from rejection:

> She had stopped teaching because of pain: she had gone with passion to high school students, year after year, and always there was one student, or even five, who wanted to feel a poem or story or novel, and see more clearly because of it. But Emily's passion dissolved in the other students. They were young and robust, and although she knew their apathy was above all a sign of their being confined by classrooms and adolescence, it still felt like apathy. It made Emily feel isolated and futile.[5]

---

[5]Andre Dubus, "Dancing After Hours," quoted in Daniel P. Liston, "Love and Despair in Teaching," *Educational Theory* 50, no. 1 (2000): 84.

Liston says teaching is most vulnerable to this kind of despair when rooted in a "romantic" love, a love rooted in our own enjoyment of learning and talking about our subject area and a yearning for students to affirm and share our enjoyment. We need, he suggests, an "enlarged love" that extends beyond our own need to be heard. We need a love ethically grounded beyond the self and capable of being sustained through suffering if we are to sustain hope in the classroom.

The challenge here has to do with more than attrition. Doris Santoro, for example, draws a useful distinction between burnout and demoralization. Burnout arises from intensifying responsibilities and demands. Demoralization has more to do with moral sources of dissatisfaction. In Santoro's words, it "derives from teachers' inability to enact the values that motivate and sustain their work."[6] It "signals a state in which teachers can no longer access the moral sources of satisfaction that made their work worthwhile."[7] Santoro presents a series of case studies of demoralized teachers, focusing on ways in which school or state policies placed them in positions where they did not feel they could do the right thing for their students, or where the behavior of school leadership eroded their sense of dignity and competence.[8] Their responses vary. Some dig in and protest or disobey. Others put their heads down and follow the rules, cutting corners as necessary, joining those who seemed content with the unreflective demands of a prescribed routine.

Santoro notes that "teachers who come to their work with significant moral purpose or those who operate with a strong sense of professional ethics are more likely to experience demoralization than teachers who have a more functional approach to their work."[9] When we raise the moral stakes of teaching, we are more likely to feel the pain of falling short. Available defense mechanisms include settling for routines of

---

[6]Doris A. Santoro, *Demoralized: Why Teachers Leave the Profession They Love and How They Can Stay* (Cambridge, MA: Harvard Education Press, 2021), 43.
[7]Santoro, *Demoralized*, 49.
[8]Santoro stresses that while burnout may be something the individual can ameliorate through lifestyle changes, demoralization is often fed by systemic issues beyond the individual's control and is a pointer to the need for changes at a larger scale.
[9]Santoro, *Demoralized*, 53.

efficiency, merely covering the material, downplaying potential, talking up the shortcomings of students, and aiming only for what we know we can most often compel them to do. Hope for more seems elusive and potentially painful.

TEACHING AS HOPE

By way of contrast, I turn to a characteristically helpful little essay titled "The Peculiar Hope of the Educator" by Nicholas Wolterstorff.[10] He begins by offering a summary of Aquinas's delineation of the nature of hope in the *Summa Theologica*.[11] I cannot beat it for succinctness and so I quote it here in full:

> Hope, says Aquinas, is a special form of desire. It is unlike *fear* in that the object is a good of some sort—or at least something that the agent regards as a good. It is unlike *joy* in that its object is a future good, whereas the object of joy is a present good. It is unlike the desire for small things in that, in Aquinas' words, its "object is something arduous and difficult to obtain." We do not "speak of anyone hoping for trifles which are in one's power to have at any time." And it is unlike *despair* in that "this difficult thing is something possible to obtain: for one does not hope for that which one cannot get at all."[12]

As he weaves together the threads binding hope to teaching, Wolterstorff goes on to argue that "aiming to teach someone is inherently an act of love, specifically, an act of benevolence."[13] He is not simply saying that the act of teaching should ideally be accompanied by benevolence or love toward our students. The point is that benevolence is intrinsic to the nature of teaching. To aim to teach is to aim at enhancing a good in the lives of students; seeking to enhance goods in others' lives is an act of benevolence. This also means teaching involves hope. The act of teaching entails hoping that the good being sought will be realized. Loss of hope

---

[10]Nicholas Wolterstorff, "The Peculiar Hope of the Educator," in *Foundations of Education: A Christian Vision*, ed. Matthew Etherington (Eugene, OR: Wipf & Stock, 2014).
[11]In citing this generalized account, I do not intend to invoke the full machinery of Aquinas's account of the dynamics of human emotions and theological virtues.
[12]Wolterstorff, "Peculiar Hope," 120.
[13]Wolterstorff, "Peculiar Hope," 122.

may show through if we habitually shy away from seeking difficult goods or settle for controlling small things.

It follows that those who aim at nothing more than presenting the material are, in Wolterstorff's stark evaluation, "not teachers; they are not trying to teach."[14] He reaches this conclusion by focusing on the triggers of our disappointment. If the aim is presenting the material, disappointment will arise if something prevents us from getting to the end of the material; the aim is merely to have enough time to finish, to feel as if we covered everything. But if our aim is to teach someone, to bring about the desired change in their learning, then disappointment is tied to the failure to achieve the intended good in the life of the student. Teaching is inherently about seeking the good of others. Presenting the material is not inherently so. Coverage and teaching have different disappointments and therefore different aims. A loss of hope may therefore manifest itself precisely in the form of allowing coverage of the material to become the dominant goal.

Let's think a little more about this idea of teaching as seeking various goods in the lives of others. It does not follow that every kind of good that students might experience should be sought by the teacher with equal energy. Fear that talk of seeking deeper goods through teaching commits us to being equally responsible for everything in students' lives can animate the common modern desire to severely curtail the list of goods that it might be proper to address. It may be suggested that we can aim for improvement at math or understanding of Shakespeare or marketable skills, but that the pursuit of moral or spiritual goods is not the teacher's job—that the academic calling is to train the mind, not to provide moral or spiritual formation. As Stanley Fish puts it, we should save the world on our own time and leave the classroom to focus on mediating disciplinary content and skills.[15]

Such cautions are driven by reasonable concerns, including the risk of indoctrination, the downsides of an educational savior complex, a concern for the rights of parents, and a worry that educational settings

---

[14]Wolterstorff, "Peculiar Hope," 123.
[15]Stanley Fish, *Save the World on Your Own Time* (New York: Oxford University Press, 2008).

are easily subverted by group agendas extrinsic to learning. There is more here than I can begin to address in this essay (or than I could adequately address given boundless time and space). For present purposes, however, I will content myself with the observation that it is normal, perhaps even unavoidable in complex human activities, to be driven by some focal hopes and goods and yet still hope for and act to realize a whole range of goods at once.

Suppose, by way of illustration, someone opens a paint factory near where I live. Suppose, over time, it becomes apparent that culpable failures of investment and management led to the factory polluting the local water supply, with damaging health consequences for people living in the area. If the factory leaders are brought to account, it will not suffice to say "but my proper purpose is to manufacture paint and make money; environmental well-being and community health are not my job." We can properly hold the leaders responsible for their impact on a wider set of goods, not just for whether they fulfilled their central purposes.

Those wider goods do not supplant the factory's focal purpose, nor do they confer omnicompetence. No one expects the factory to abandon the paint business and become a conservation program. We are unlikely to reason that because the process of paint manufacture can have health consequences, the factory managers should take over running the local clinic. But none of this implies that the wider goods are irrelevant to the making of paint. Those wider goods should be actively hoped for, with corresponding planning and investment, by those who make paint. The wider goods become part of what makes the paint-making good.

So with teaching. Our focal goal may be to teach chemistry. It does not follow that in doing so we have no impact on other goods. Nor does it follow that we have no responsibility to do what is within our power to work toward the realization of other goods. We can be held responsible for all of the effects of our teaching. More than one way exists to teach any given matter; we have choices to make. Those choices will say something about our hopes, which are related to the particular goods in which we want to invest. I hope to show that this is so by turning now to more concrete depictions of teaching practices rooted in specific hopes.

HOPE AND COMMUNITY

In the interests of hastening our journey from philosophical consider-
ations to the habits of the classroom, I propose to narrow our focus to
one kind of good for which the Christian tradition has nurtured hope.
It is not the only one, but it is quite central and will serve as a place to
focus our attention here. What Paul called "the hope of the glory of God"
(Rom 5:2 NIV) involves more than the possibility of salvation for individuals. The working of grace includes incorporation into a new kind of
community grounded neither in individual self-assertion nor in kinship-
based solidarity. Redemption involves the building of disparate people
into a new body, a new temple, a new fellowship. One pithy summary of
what is now to be both hoped for and practiced can be found in section
26 of the Westminster Confession:[16]

> All saints that are united to Jesus Christ their head, by His Spirit and by
> faith, have fellowship with Him in His graces, sufferings, death, resur-
> rection, and glory: and, being united to one another in love, they have
> communion in each other's gifts and graces, and are obliged to the per-
> formance of such duties, public and private, as do conduce to their mutual
> good, both in the inward and outward man. Saints, by profession, are
> bound to maintain an holy fellowship and communion in the worship of
> God, and in performing such other spiritual services as tend to their
> mutual edification; as also in relieving each other in outward things, ac-
> cording to their several abilities and necessities.

The hope expressed here is that in Christ we might live out of and into a
form of human community in which our commitment to one another
does not arise from sharing the same gender, politics, musical tastes,
ethnicity, or neighborhood, but is built upon God's choice to welcome
us in Christ. Such a hope entails active responsibilities and practices: we
are "obliged" to the "performance of duties," with the content of those
duties being whatever contributes to the mutual good.

---

[16]A document produced by the 1646 Westminster Assembly to serve as a confessional framework
for the Church of England. See, e.g., The Westminster Confession of Faith, Ligonier, www
.ligonier.org/learn/articles/westminster-confession-faith.

This vision of community includes shared "worship" and "spiritual services," but it does not stop there. It includes "relieving each other in outward things," things both "public and private." The hope is not primarily that we will enjoy congenial company, but that we will commit ("obliged," "duties," "bound") to one another's good. The ground is neither our personal inclination nor our ability to secure and control the desired outcome, but the prior commitment to our collective good enacted and being completed in Christ.

Such a passage is, of course, a terse summary of more textured biblical and theological sources. We could refer, for instance, to Galatians 5 and 6, where Paul affirms that "the only thing that counts is faith expressing itself through love" (Gal 5:6 NIV). The series of contrasts that Paul then draws between indulging the flesh and walking by the Spirit are disproportionately focused on the ability to dwell together in love. The pattern of "not," "so," and "however" in these chapters pits mutual service and love of neighbor against various forms of self-preoccupation and hostility. "Therefore," he concludes, "as we have opportunity, let us do good to all people" (Gal 6:10 NIV). As John Barclay notes in a detailed discussion of this passage, the focus on mutual service here is not merely an ethics section appended to the central theology, but rather describes the necessary expression of the gift of Christ worked out in the "creation and development of communities governed by new values and norms."[17]

We could also turn to broader theological sources. Dietrich Bonhoeffer emphasized a contrast between our dream of experienced community and the actual community called into being in Christ. He emphasized that "Christianity means community through Jesus Christ and in Jesus Christ. No Christian community is more or less than this. . . . We belong to one another only through and in Jesus Christ."[18] If we allow this ground to be replaced by our romantic visions of friction-free fellowship, Bonhoeffer warns, we are likely to quickly become disappointed with the actual people with whom we have been placed in fellowship.

---

[17]John M. G. Barclay, *Paul and the Power of Grace* (Grand Rapids, MI: Eerdmans, 2020), 64.
[18]Dietrich Bonhoeffer, *Life Together and Prayerbook of the Bible*. Dietrich Bonhoeffer Works, vol. 5, trans. James H. Burtness and Daniel W. Bloesch (Minneapolis: Fortress, 1996).

They will fall short of our dream. Despair at the failure of our romantic longings will be expressed in indignation. Before long we will become their embittered accusers.[19]

Each of these sources, with many others like them, expresses a hope for a community of mutual edification founded in mutual care and service. At first blush, it seems that in sketching this hope, we drifted away from the affairs of the classroom. The hope in these sources is theological. It reaches toward God's agency in creating a new humanity in Christ. This is not something to be secured by better teaching strategies.

Yet even without articulating a full account of how grace and human agency or theological and mundane hopes interact, it seems worth noting that the theological sources here do not speak as if the necessity of grace or the primacy of God's agency entail quietism. Instead, they articulate a realism about the work entailed and a call to express hope in active labor. We should seek to do good "as we have opportunity," wrote Paul (Gal 6:10 NIV).

Such an understanding is also reflected in various Christian confessions. For example, the Westminster Confession urges us to consider the active "duties" that we become bound to perform because of our having been united in Christ. As the Belhar Confession puts it, our reconciliation to one another is "both a gift and an obligation for the church of Jesus Christ; that through the working of God's Spirit it is a binding force, yet simultaneously a reality which must be earnestly pursued and sought," with the proviso that "unity can be established only in freedom and not under constraint."[20] Hope is meant to lapse into neither self-gratifying yearning nor feats of control; it is meant to ground patient practice directed toward what has been promised. Theological hope creates a horizon toward which our mundane hopes and worldly energies are to be pointed.

---

[19]Bonhoeffer, *Life Together*, 34-35. For examples of application of Bonhoeffer's account of community practices to teaching, see David I. Smith, *On Christian Teaching: Practicing Faith in the Classroom* (Grand Rapids, MI: Eerdmans, 2018), 97-113, and the literature cited there.

[20]*The Belhar Confession*, Reformed Church in America, at www.rca.org/about/theology/creeds -and-confessions/the-belhar-confession/, 2.

This focus on dependent duties suggests that it is not at all improper to ask how our hopes for the classroom might intersect with this endeavor. What kind of educational practices might prove consistent with hoping for the "difficult thing" of living toward this kind of community, while remaining focused on the importance of more quotidian learning goals and avoiding both romantic dreaming and cynical control?

Leaning into Community

I have been thinking for some years about how to structure my classes to emphasize *communion in one another's gifts and graces* and the hope for a life together grounded in the gift and obligation of seeking one another's good. I began to make this explicit in my course syllabi. Here is one example from a course on world language pedagogy:

> Learning to think deeply entails paying attention to and learning from those around us. The best teaching does not grow out of solitary reflection. This course will therefore include an emphasis on collaboration. Success means not just getting your own tasks done but helping those around you to become better learners and teachers, so that more of the needs of their future students will be met. This is an important way in which you can begin to serve those students now as well as honoring the gifts and needs that each other participant brings to the class. As we work at collaborating on transformative educational practices, we will have opportunities to try to do *justice* to the ideas of others, exercise *patience* with their learning process, offer our own ideas with *humility* (which means not thinking too highly of ourselves but also being willing to share ideas openly). Our goal is not to win arguments. It is to figure out how teaching languages can be a work of love.

Including such prose in the syllabus could easily be little more than romantic aspiration, especially if the syllabus is broadcast to students for passive consumption and followed by business as usual. If, however, the syllabus can be turned into what Quentin Schultze calls a "covenant syllabus,"[21] one that articulates a shared rule of life that is negotiated with

---

[21]Quentin Schultze, *Servant Teaching: Practices for Renewing Christian Higher Education* (Grand Rapids, MI: Edenridge Press, 2022), 74.

students and includes expectations for the instructor, it can become an initial orientation to hopeful practice. The syllabus is not merely a communication of boundaries to students. It is an initial public commitment on my part to fostering the kind of teaching and learning practices that might make the language of the syllabus have an effect on our work together.

One way I have approached grounding the syllabus themes is to explicitly structure interaction around mutual care. On the first day of the semester, I begin with an activity that focuses not just on students introducing themselves to me, but also on their learning something about one another.[22] A week or two later, when the cognitive demands of the first days have settled a little, I introduce the idea of accountability groups. I assign students to groups of four (or the best approximation based on class numbers). These groups are intentionally not based upon affinity networks, though I do sometimes find it helpful to base them on shared vocational trajectories (such as an intended teaching career focus in terms of subject or grade level). I communicate explicitly my reasons for not forming friendship-based groups. These groups are an opportunity to explore a less individualistic learning culture and to work at an active commitment to another's good that responds to grace rather than preference. I ask group members to commit to small, achievable ways of seeking one another's good, providing examples to prompt imagination. If one group member does not show up for class, the others should be the first to notice and to contact that person to offer help or class notes. If one group member begins to struggle academically or personally during the semester, others should notice and see if they can offer support or nudge them toward me or relevant student services. If we are heading into demanding phases of the semester, such as midterms, that might be a good time for an encouraging word, a supporting prayer. The actions chosen should not be ones that unreasonably increase the workload, nor should they be efforts to impress. They should be small ways of leaning into the awareness of others as recipients of grace.

---

[22]I elaborate on this in David I. Smith, *Everyday Christian Teaching* (Grand Rapids, MI: Eerdmans, forthcoming). I describe another example of such an activity in detail in Smith, *On Christian Teaching*, 14-26.

To avoid this exhortation becoming one more airy aspiration, I check in with students at intervals and provide regular learning activities that draw the group members into interaction. About once a week a learning activity asks the group to collaborate. The task might be a brief discussion based on a shared core reading supplemented by each group member reading a different additional piece and sharing what it could add to the group's understanding. It might focus on weighing a key idea from class and submitting a joint paragraph summarizing the group's reactions and questions.

I am, however, mindful of two potential obstacles. Students live in varied locations and have complex schedules, so tasks requiring lengthy meetings outside class will be disproportionately burdensome. Students also describe to me a common tendency for their teachers to assign group projects focused on product rather than process, resulting almost inevitably in the work being divided up and assembled at the last minute, making the group activity essentially a series of parallel solo projects but with the added stress of relying on others' promptness.

With those obstacles in mind, I focus the tasks on processing ideas together and keep the time necessary to complete them down to fifteen or twenty minutes, with time, if needed, assigned in class. This is not the only group configuration. Other class activities create space for students to learn with and from those outside their group. I offer periodic reminders that we are seeking ways for every class member to experience being supported by at least three others, rather than leaving the degree of mutual support experienced to the varying strength of each person's networks and abilities. We are seeking a way in which all class members can commit to serving those around them regardless of how deserving they seem. Like the content of the class, this is something we will work at together, confessing when we fall short and periodically revisiting our progress. At the end of the semester, I debrief with students in focus groups.[23]

This is not a technique for fixing students' failings or ensuring academic success. I work to frame it for students as an invitation into

---

[23]See David I. Smith, "Reflections on How to End a Semester," *Christian Scholars Review Blog,* December 2, 2020, at https://christianscholars.com/reflections-on-how-to-end-a-semester/.

intentional practice, practice that may go well or poorly, practice that must be open to grace, the kind of practice that pushes back a little against the ingrained patterns of our formation and invites us to hope for and perhaps live into more than what is familiar. It adds minimal time to my teaching load, and I find that it contributes to rather than subtracts from the time spent learning course content.

Most of my students are Christian. Over the years that I have been doing this, I have found students generally willing to embrace the practice and appreciative of its rationale. That does not mean instant harmony. Last year one student wrote eloquently at the end of the semester about how she could work more efficiently and get better grades alone, and it made life more convenient to do so. Yet she concluded that by the end of the semester she realized perhaps the most important thing she learned at university that semester was what she could gain from working with others.

This is, of course, just one student's experience, but it is suggestive of the proper arc of sustained practice. This kind of practice is a leaning in the same direction over time, a gradual and partial living into hope for supportive community in response to the promises that ground such a hope.

Building Toward Community

I turn to the classrooms of my colleagues in the natural sciences for a second example. The lone genius in a warren of arcane equipment may be a recurring media trope, but science is not typically done alone. Teams of scientists with varying disciplinary tools and concepts, as well as the usual range of human differences and failings, need to function well together to get complex scientific work done. The recently established field of the science of team science investigates how such collaboration flourishes and founders.[24]

Rachael Baker and Amy Wilstermann, science faculty at Calvin University, decided to explore how the science of team science might connect

---

[24]See, e.g., Daniel Stokols, Kara L. Hall, Brandie K. Taylor, and Richard P. Moser, "The Science of Team Science: Overview of the Field and Introduction to the Supplement," *American Journal of Preventive Medicine* 35, no. 2 Supplement (2008): S77-S89.

with the practices of intentional Christian communities. Through interviews and site visits, they identified practices that seemed to play a constructive role in enabling such communities to function. Those practices included hospitality, humility, learning together, self-reflection, gratitude, silence, and rest. Identifying these as practices, rather than as values or aspirations, enabled a bridge to science classroom practices and the creation of science courses framed by intentional relational practice.

Wilstermann writes that "equipping students with an understanding of the collaborative nature of science helps them to recognize and value the individual contributions of team members who bring a variety of skill sets, insights, and experiences to their work."[25] Baker and Wilstermann developed an instructional process that included discussion of what each practice means, opportunities to experiment with the practice, and then discussion of its effects on learning and belonging. Each of these phases was important for the learning process.

Take humility as an example. Julie Yonker, a psychologist who helped evaluate the project, describes how the process began with discussion of what we might mean by humility in a science lab and what behaviors might be related to it.[26] Those behaviors might include asking for help instead of pretending competence, listening to others with the expectation of learning from them, and being honest and realistic about one's capacities.

In a Christian classroom, the context for such behaviors includes awareness of our creaturely dependence and our call to charity toward others. Once shared understanding is established, students are asked to select a practice from a number of alternatives and focus on pursuing it for a week. For instance,

- At least once a week during class (either as part of the whole class or during a small group discussion), ask a question to the professor/teacher or a peer about something you don't understand.

[25]Amy Wilstermann, "Building Thriving Science Laboratory and Classroom Communities," *Christian Educators Journal* 62, no. 1 (October 2022): 12.

[26]Julie E. Yonker, "Could Humility Be the Heart of Our Classroom Communities?," *Christian Educators Journal* 62, no. 1 (October 2022): 22. There are relevant discussions to be had here about how procedural definitions of humility relate to thicker theological definitions; for present purposes I am merely noting how a particular faith-grounded hope, however expressed, can inform teaching.

- Admit when you do not know something, do not understand something, or do not know how to do something (do not pretend to have knowledge or abilities that you lack).
- Admit mistakes when they occur, rather than hide/ignore them.
- Ask for help when you need it.
- Display patience when others ask for help, or admit they do not understand something, or tell you that they have made a mistake, recognizing that these acts require humility (and courage).[27]

Next, students were invited to reflect on their experience of the practice and its effects on their learning, using questions such as these:

- Was this practice comfortable or uncomfortable for you? How did it change your experience in the classroom/lab?
- Why is humility important in community?
- Is humility a virtue that is valuable in leaders?
- Are there limits to the value of admitting mistakes, acknowledging lack of knowledge?
- Does humility have a place in competitive settings? If so, what does humility look like in an environment where prestige and recognition matter?[28]

Preliminary data gathered from students suggest gains in intellectual humility as well as gains in terms of regular science learning.[29] Student reflections convey something of their own perceived growth. "When looking back at my experience in the classroom, humility changed my orientation from me-focused to group-focused," wrote one student. Another reported: "I also noticed that I was a happier person while intentionally practicing humility. The prideful mentality is a heavy load to carry while being a college student."[30] A third student noted that "being

---

[27]Yonker, "Humility," 22.
[28]Yonker, "Humility," 23.
[29]See also Julie E. Yonker, Adrienne R. Pendery, Christopher Klein, and John Witte, "Relational-Based Christian Practices of Gratitude and Prayer Can Positively Impact Christian College Students' Reported Prosocial Tendencies," *International Journal of Christianity and Education* 23, no. 2 (2019): 150-70.
[30]Yonker, "Humility," 24.

humble has elevated my learning experience because now, I get the chance to hear other people's thoughts and ideas as well as how they have come to their conclusion."[31]

Such student comments hint at how intentional relational practices might enhance rather than compete with the conventional task of learning science. As one instructor noted, "A classroom of humble individuals also creates efficiencies in how a classroom or team functions, namely, students are more willing to ask questions and be vulnerable in their learning which makes it easier for the teacher to address areas of confusion, thereby saving time."[32] Pursuing the goods of mutually supportive community enhanced the ability to work well with others, listen well to others, communicate clearly and honestly, and request and receive input from collaborators.

Here we bump once more into questions of hope and control. The findings reported so far from this experiment suggest that the common faculty instinct that sees investment in formational goals or intentional relational practices as time stolen from covering the course material is a misperception. A faith-informed hope for *more* need not compete with getting things done. At the same time, the focus on virtues such as humility and hospitality seems likely to become self-undermining if such virtues come to be seen as merely instrumental for improving the efficiency of science instruction.

This tension is not unusual, however. It seems we can turn just about anything, prayer and worship included, into a routinely managed substitute for genuine hope and dependence on grace. Yet turning away from such practices is not the answer. Does the framing vision for a course involve the pursuit of *communion in one another's gifts and graces* in light of what Christ promised and accomplished? Or is it merely a quest for variables affecting course coverage? The answer matters. It matters what kind of hope frames the habits.

---

[31] Rachael Baker, "What Faith Has to Offer Science," *Christian Educators Journal* 62, no. 1 (October 2022): 3.
[32] Yonker, "Humility," 24.

PRACTICES OF HOPE

I suggest the practices described above are best framed as efforts to lean hopefully into teaching as an act of benevolence. Those who invest in such practices dare to seek goods deeper than content coverage and test scores, and they dare to imagine that the larger and smaller goods can be pursued together rather than being approached as a zero-sum game. These practices are examples of educational habits that are "unlike the desire for small things," focusing instead on matters that are "arduous and difficult to obtain" and yet "possible to obtain."[33] As habits of hope, they seem to me to live in a space between at least two undesirable options. One is the despair that might lead us to perceive the complex humanity of students and the breadth of Christian hope as obstacles to efficient performance and to settle for routinely controllable learning outcomes. The other is the airy optimism that might see us treating goods such as community and humility as matters for exhortation and aspiration in the classroom yet failing to invest in intentionally and patiently sustained practices and shared narratives that might support their growth.

Especially in our current pedagogical culture, practices like the ones described here could be misread as attempts at control, attempts to secure the goods envisioned in New Testament and confessional language through the application of pedagogical technique. We might then be replacing the hopes characteristic of Christian eschatology by educational fixes, which could in the end be one more way of settling for what we can control.[34] After all, the Scriptures and confessions ground the hope of a new community in Christ rather than in good lesson planning.

Furthermore, if the hopes described here turn into one more technique of control or into romantic visions of unfailingly harmonious classrooms and virtuous students, by raising the stakes of teaching through the naming of larger goods we may be inviting a fresh despair. As Santoro noted, those with the grandest ethical visions may often become the most demoralized.

---

[33]Wolterstorff, "Peculiar Hope," 120.
[34]See Richard Bauckham and Trevor Hart, *Hope Against Hope: Christian Eschatology at the Turn of the Millennium* (Grand Rapids, MI: Eerdmans, 1999).

Another story, however, is possible. That story would read practices like those described here not as techniques of behavioral manipulation, but as narratively framed ways of inviting students into hopeful practices and exploring the complex consequences for students' overall growth and self-understanding. It would note (like the theological sources touched on earlier) that grounding hope in God's gracious intervention and invitation to a new way of life does not negate the validity of intentional or even confident efforts to live toward that hope. As James K. A. Smith puts it, "hope differs from a guarantee, even though it is also characterized by a certain confidence."[35] Living out of that confidence, we should "make every effort" to add goodness to our faith (2 Pet 1:5). Such effort is not merely individual; we can pursue the kinds of goods described here in terms of our own character and that of our students and also in terms of our shared hope for the goods of grace-sustained community in our life together.

In all of this, our effort needs a better ground than romantic love. Liston suggests teaching can be sustained only by an "enlarged love," a love larger than our own desires for fulfillment in the classroom. Such love needs to be rooted beyond the self, in goods that exceed us and in attentiveness to the stake that others have in those goods.[36] Seen within a Christian frame, it must be a grateful love of God and neighbor that reaches beyond our need for others to gratify our preferences. If we are rooted in such a love, we might approach the mundane task of teaching within the context of hope for all things made new, accepting God's promises as having a solidity that makes them a proper ground for action.[37] The possibility emerges here of a resistance to despair that is not dependent on our students' or our schools' immediate perfectibility.

This has been, of course, a fragmentary account. The examples here are just examples. The goods of community are not the only difficult

---

[35]James K. A. Smith, "Determined Hope: A Phenomenology of Christian Expectation," in *The Future of Hope: Christian Tradition amid Modernity and Postmodernity*, ed. Miroslav Volf and William Katerberg (Grand Rapids, MI: Eerdmans, 2004), 209.

[36]Drawing upon Iris Murdoch, Liston describes "enlarged love" as involving "a diminished sense of self, an attentive gaze toward the situation and the other, and a presumption that 'good' exists and is the object of love." Liston, "Love and Despair," 95.

[37]Smith, "Determined Hope," 208.

goods that Christian hope might illuminate, though they are essential to Christian hope. In pursuing such goods, there is much more to address than the choices of the individual teacher, embedded as all teaching is in systemic institutional and cultural processes. In seeking transformation and discerning the geography of grace and presumption, we reckon with the complexities of the teacher's own heart and motives as well as those of our students.

I have merely attempted to concretely illustrate a few basic intuitions. Teaching is beset, especially now but perhaps always, by the temptation to despair. Hope is most like itself when it exerts a formative influence on our mundane daily practices. It is denatured when reduced to lofty rhetoric or romantic yearning or replaced by control. Teachers can and should hope for more than covering required material and getting students through the exam. This need not be incompatible with desiring to teach all the material or get students through the exam. Teaching practices grounded in the intentional pursuit of benevolent but difficult goods can help sustain hope as well as arise from hope. Hope can become a pedagogical habit.

—CONCLUSION—

THE HABITAT OF HOPE

Jon S. Kulaga

Hope also requires a life corresponding to the hope.

St. John of Kronstadt, *My Life in Christ*

As Cleopas and his friend make the seven-mile trek back to Emmaus following the crucifixion and resurrection of Jesus, they are "talking with each other about everything that had happened" (Lk 24:14, NIV throughout). Along the way, a stranger joins them and enters the conversation. Later, of course, we find out that this stranger is none other than Jesus himself in his post-resurrected state.

Feigning ignorance, Jesus enquires about the topic—or person—they are so intently discussing, to which Cleopas responds in amazement, "Are you the only one visiting Jerusalem who does not know the things that have happened there in these days?" (Lk 24:18). After giving this stranger a brief overview of what we now call the Passion Week, Cleopas ends his summary with the words, "But we had hoped that he was the one who was going to redeem Israel" (24:21).

Jesus then proceeds to walk the rest of the way to Emmaus, teaching and explaining what Moses and the prophets said about the Messiah and how it all intersects and converges in the life, death, and resurrection of the Nazarene whom they had been following. Upon arriving in Emmaus, Jesus pretends he needs to go on farther but is persuaded by his new friends to come in for a meal and rest, even for the night. As he breaks bread for the meal, the eyes of the two travelers are opened, recognizing Jesus standing before them—who then vanishes.

HOSPITALITY: THE HABITAT OF HOPE

In this short narrative in the Gospel of Luke, we see many of the habits of hope discussed in this volume fleshed out in the lives of the two disciples. These include the conversation between friends and a mentor, as well as diversity in that while Cleopas is a common male Greek name, the other traveler could very well have been Jewish and could have been female. Greek men and Jewish women were not uncommon among Jesus' followers. They came to understand the unfolding of all the Scriptures they had read from childhood and wrote about in school and listened to teachers explain, all within the context, or habitat, of hospitality.

Considering this theme, Christine Pohl offers that "hospitality often involves small deaths and little resurrections."[1] This understanding is especially true in the previously noted example of hospitality that involved a big death and an even bigger resurrection. Hospitality is the habitat of grace that makes the other habits incubate and thrive. Pohl thus notes, "By God's grace, we can grow more willing, more eager, to open the door to a needy neighbor or a stranger in distress."[2] Within the habitat of hospitality, we gradually become more sensitive to and more aware of the fact that due to the busyness and pace with which we live our lives, we have thrown our neighbor out with the bathwater of ingratitude.

In another of her works, *Friendship at the Margins: Discovering Mutuality in Service and Mission*, Pohl, along with coauthor Christopher Heuertz, contends that real friendship (and hospitality) involves movement in and out of another person's world. Sometimes because of our privilege or status we don't even see possible friends who, though not far away, are distant from us.

---

[1] Christine D. Pohl, *Making Room: Recovering Hospitality as a Christian Tradition* (Grand Rapids, MI: Eerdmans, 1999), 187.
[2] Pohl, *Making Room*, 187.

The Christian university is a unique place where both faculty and students inhabit spaces in which they can meet people unlike themselves. The pace of the semester, especially in the residential college experience, hopefully allows both the teacher and the student to slow down. Slowing down allows "taking time to be where people can befriend us, and taking risks to be dependent on the kindness of strangers."[3] They hopefully also find "opportunities for friendships that cross multiple boundaries if we would just notice them."[4]

There is a difference between good teaching and great teaching, just like there is a difference between service and hospitality in a restaurant. This distinction is creatively pointed out by Will Guidara, the former owner of the three-Michelin Star restaurant Eleven Madison Park, in *Unreasonable Hospitality*: "Getting the right plate to the right person at the table is service. But genuinely engaging with the person you are serving, so you can make an authentic connection—that's hospitality."[5] In another place, he observes that "service is black and white, while hospitality is color."[6] This is true of average teaching versus implementing the habits of hope outlined in this book.

To paraphrase Will Guidera, we might offer that getting the right lecture with the right information on the right day delivered to the right students is average teaching (service). But genuinely engaging the entire class in a meaningful conversation on the subject, from a diversity of perspectives and learning modalities facilitating authentic connections, is great teaching. A classroom focused on service can effectively transmit information. A classroom imbued with a sense of hospitality, however, creates a habitat in which all the habits hope can live and flourish. One is black and white. The other is color.

THE END OF HABITS

The road to Emmaus story is also a good reminder that our survey of the habits of hope in higher education confronts us with the question,

---

[3]Christopher L. Heuertz and Christine D. Pohl, *Friendship at the Margins: Discovering Mutuality in Service and Mission* (Downers Grove, IL: InterVarsity Press, 2010), 130-31.
[4]Heuertz and Pohl, *Friendship at the Margins*, 131.
[5]Will Guidara, *Unreasonable Hospitality: The Remarkable Power of Giving People More Than They Expect* (New York: Optimism Press, 2022), 5.
[6]Guidara, *Unreasonable Hospitality*, 5.

Toward what end? What is the purpose of all the walking and talking?
All the eating and drinking? What is the purpose of opening their minds
to further understanding? Likewise, what is the purpose of integration,
conversation, reading, writing, and teaching? Why bother with efforts
toward racial and ethnic reconciliation and diversity?

A hint of an answer is found in the reaction of the two disciples when
Jesus vanished in front of their eyes, as reported in Luke 24:30-34:

> When he was at the table with them, he took bread, gave thanks, broke it
> and began to give it to them. Then their eyes were opened and they rec-
> ognized him, and he disappeared from their sight. They asked each other,
> "Were not our hearts burning within us while he talked with us on the road
> and opened the Scriptures to us?"
>
> They got up and returned at once to Jerusalem. There they found the
> Eleven and those with them, assembled together and saying, "It is true!
> The Lord has risen." (Luke 24:30-34)

Like Olympic race walkers caught between a walk and a run, the end of
the passage sees our once-despairing disciples winding their way back to
Jerusalem in the darkness to reaffirm what the disciples who stayed
behind already knew—Jesus was *alive!*

The purpose of the habits of hope (walking, talking, eating, drinking,
and opening their minds to understand the Scriptures) was not for the
two disciples' self-edification. When Jesus vanished into thin air, they did
not retire for the evening pondering these things in their hearts. They hit
the road! Why? Because if Jesus was alive, they had found their purpose,
and they had work to do!

I suppose it's cliché to write that despair is often camouflaged by activity. Rather than waiting, it's best to be off going somewhere—even
anywhere. Søren Kierkegaard wrote in *The Sickness unto Death* that the
specific character of despair is precisely being unaware of being in despair.[7] The disciples left Jerusalem with their hopes crushed. "We had
hoped"—past tense.

---

[7]Søren Kierkegaard, *The Sickness unto Death: A Christian Psychological Exposition for Upbuilding
and Awakening*, trans. Howard V. Hong and Edna H. Hong (Princeton, NJ: Princeton University
Press, 1983).

The road to Emmaus was one of *desperation.*
But the road to back Jerusalem was one of *discernment.*
He is alive.
The first trip was made in *pain.*
The second trip was made with *purpose.*
The end of the fourteen-mile round trip was a renewed sense of purpose and vision to declare to any who had ears to hear, "Jesus is alive!" This was their hope. In the months and years ahead, many who held on to this hope and shared it with others would lose their lives as martyrs, but they died to a living hope.

In his work *Visons of Vocation,* Steven Garber writes, "Good societies anywhere require people with a . . . sense of calling . . . who see into the messes and horrors and complexities of human history and decide to enter in for justice's sake."[8] It is for the purpose of being salt and light, sheep among wolves, ambassadors for Christ, that we give a winsome defense for the hope within. It is to offer ourselves as living sacrifices that we practice these habits of hope. It is for the end of witnessing a mess but seeing an opportunity for ministry.

In *The End of Education,* Neil Postman questions whether American culture still believes in the ideal school, especially public schools, when a coherent and cohesive understanding of what constitutes the public no longer exists.[9] Similarly, for us to believe in the efficacy of habits of hope that an unapologetically Christ-centered college education can exhibit, we must first believe in the efficacy of, and need for, a college education. What is the "end" toward which it is striving? Why even bother with hope while one is trying to navigate through the labyrinthian halls of higher education? In the final pages, Postman offers up his vision of education in "good faith" but not with "much confidence."[10]

Hope, however, is not faith. The two disciples had faith. They had just lost hope. Faith believes God can. Hope believes God will. The issue on

[8]Steven Garber, *Visions of Vocation: Common Grace for the Common Good* (Downers Grove, IL: InterVarsity Press, 2014), 44.
[9]Neil Postman, *The End of Education: Redefining the Value of School* (New York: Knopf, 1995).
[10]Postman, *End of Education,* 196.

the Emmaus road is not faith. The issue is hope. Practicing the habits of hope requires faith, and as hope grows, faith deepens.

Repeating the quote from Peter Mommsen noted in the introduction:

> The resurrected Jesus—a flesh-and-blood person who in the Gospels eats a meal, breaks bread . . . is proof and pioneer of what humankind will be. . . . In the interim of the ages, as the universe's great Sabbath approaches, humankind has work to do. . . . The times may be troubled but beyond them, there's a future to eagerly await.[11]

This is the purpose of practicing the habits of hope in our classrooms, recital halls, libraries, residence halls, dining commons, and even on basketball courts. It is to weave together a purpose in life grounded in a belief in truth that is "coherent across the whole of life, because it addresses the whole of life," this life and the next.[12] It is to ground the student in a purpose that is predicated upon God being not only able (faith), but also willing (hope). It is to aid our students in developing "a life corresponding to the hope" we harbor.[13]

AN END NOTE—ON ESCHATOLOGY

It is apropos to save the last word for last things as hope has always assumed an eschatology, an end that invigorates. Q: Why do athletes practice? A: Game day. Q: Why do students attend classes, take tests, and write papers? A: Graduation day. Q: Why do musicians spend hours practicing the same piece repeatedly? A: Concert day.

If there was never a game, it would be difficult to motivate players to practice. If a student never graduated and college lasted forever, motivation and attendance would eventually evaporate. If a concert was never offered, the gift of music would remain unfulfilled. Why bother with hope if the "why" of life is just to grease the wheels of a machine that is

---

[11]Peter Mommsen, "From the Editor," *Plough* 32 (2022), 21.
[12]Steven Garber, *The Fabric of Faithfulness: Weaving Together Belief and Behavior* (Downers Grove, IL: InterVarsity Press, 1997), 124.
[13]St. John of Kronstadt, *My Life in Christ*, trans. E. E. Goulaeff (London: Cassell and Company, 1897), 507, https://ccel.org/ccel/kronstadt/christlife.

being driven off a cliff? For the Christian, last things have always influenced first things.

When Peter wanted to encourage the believers living in the five Roman provinces of Asia Minor not to abandon hope due to their suffering and persecution, and to "stand firm" and live honorably before a watching world, it was within the overarching context of their ultimate glorification and Christ's second coming (see 1 Pet 3). Peter's question of "How then shall we live?" is posed in light of his eschatology. Today's choices are always defined by an anticipation of tomorrow. This has been more eloquently expounded at length by others, as in Francis Schaeffer's *How Should We Then Live?* and Charles Colson and Nancy Pearcey's *How Now Shall We Live?* to name but two popular examples.

The Westminster Shorter Catechism, completed in 1647 by the Westminster Assembly, serves as the key guiding document of doctrinal standards for many in the Reformed tradition. The question-and-answer format serves as a catechizing curriculum for spiritual formation within that tradition. I believe it is instructive that the very first question deals with the end.

Q. 1. What is the chief end of man?

A. Man's chief end is to glorify God, and to enjoy him forever.[14]

Two things are striking. First, we have an end for which we have been created, "to glorify God." And second, that end alone is one that lasts forever. These are eschatological answers that inform all existential realities for the believer.

This view stands in stark contrast to the lack of hope that reverberates through Anthony Kronman's eulogy for the meaning of life and a life of meaning as a professional subject worthy of exploration at most secular universities.[15] Lacking anything outside oneself to give life meaning, the secular humanist, and as a result the secular humanities, no longer have

---

[14]*The Westminster Shorter Catechism in Modern English*, ed. Douglas F. Kelly, Philip B. Rollinson, and Frederick T. Marsh (Phillipsburg, NJ: P&R Publishing, 1986), 5.
[15]Anthony T. Kronman, *Education's End: Why Our Colleges Have Given Up on the Meaning of Life* (New Haven, CT: Yale University Press, 2007), 7.

anything of worth to offer today's university curriculum driven by the scientific-research paradigm that controls today's promotion and tenure process.

Kronman admits that questions about "ends" are essential questions, and that these questions inform any discussion about the meaning of life, as well as one's whole life. However, for the secular humanist, these questions can be answered only by placing oneself into a context larger than life itself. A context, he writes, they lack. So they "can also never be answered from a point of view that we are really never . . . able to adopt."[16]

But that is not so for the faith-informed classroom, where faith and learning are integrated. It was the great hymn writer of the eighteenth century Charles Wesley who called for believers, pastors, and professors to "unite the pair so long disjoined, / knowledge and vital piety."[17] The habits of hope are meant to produce a certain kind of life. That is the end toward which they point, the end that justifies their existence in the first place. A life that corresponds with the hope we proclaim.

---

[16]Kronman, *Education's End*, 32-33.
[17]Charles Wesley, "Come Father, Son, and Holy Ghost," United Methodist Discipleship Ministries, https://www.umcdiscipleship.org/resources/come-father-son-and-holy-ghost.

CONTRIBUTORS

Hans Boersma holds the chair to the Order of St. Benedict Servants of Christ Endowed Professorship in Ascetical Theology at Nashotah House Theological Seminary and is an ordained priest within the Anglican Church in North America. Before beginning his service at Nashotah House in 2019, Boersma taught for fourteen years at Regent College in Vancouver, British Columbia, and for six years at Trinity Western University in Langley, British Columbia. He is the author and editor of numerous books, including *Seeing God: The Beatific Vision in the Christian Tradition* and, most recently, *Pierced by Love: Divine Reading with the Christian Tradition.*

Kimberly Battle-Walters Denu is provost and dean of the faculty at Westmont College. Previously, she served as the vice president for educational programs for the Council for Christian Colleges and Universities (CCCU). She has received two Fulbright awards, one to South Africa and one to Ethiopia, and is an ordained minister who has served on six continents. She is the author of *Sheila's Shop: Working-Class African American Women Talk About Life, Love, Race, and Hair* and the editor of *Mothers Are Leaders* (with her mother, Janet S. Walters).

Christopher J. Devers is assistant professor of education at Johns Hopkins University and senior fellow for operations for the Lumen Research Institute. The author of numerous articles in leading journals, Devers is interested in applied metacognitive processes and how people learn. Specifically, he explores learning as facilitated by using videos and mobile devices in online environments. He is also interested in the scholarship of teaching and learning and student success.

Kevin G. Grove, CSC, is assistant professor of theology at the University of Notre Dame, where he also serves as an assistant faculty chaplain, chaplain to the Master of Divinity program, and pastoral resident for undergraduates in Dunne Hall. Previously, he held fellowships with L'Institut Catholique and the Notre Dame Institute for Advanced Study. He is the author of *Augustine on Memory* and the editor of *Art, Desire, and God: Phenomenological Perspectives* (with Christopher C. Rios and Taylor J. Nutter).

Cherie Harder is president of the Trinity Forum. Prior to joining the Trinity Forum in 2008, Harder served in the White House as special assistant to the president and director of policy and projects for First Lady Laura Bush. Earlier in her career, she served as policy advisor to Senate Majority Leader Bill Frist, advising the leader on domestic social issues and serving as liaison and outreach director to outside groups. From 2001 to 2005, she was senior counselor to the chairman of the National Endowment for the Humanities (NEH), where she helped the chairman design and launch the We the People initiative to enhance the teaching, study, and understanding of American history. Prior to that, Harder was the policy director for Senator Sam Brownback and served as deputy policy director at Empower America.

Jon S. Kulaga is president of Indiana Wesleyan University. Previously, Kulaga served as president of Ohio Christian University for five years, beginning in 2017. Kulaga also has served in various executive and leadership roles, including chief academic officer and chief operating officer at Asbury University, and in academics, advancement, and student life development roles at Spring Arbor University. He was an ordained deacon and elder in the Free Methodist denomination for more than thirty years before transferring his ordination to the Wesleyan denomination. He is an honorary Kentucky colonel, the author of *Edward Payson Hart: The Second Man of Free Methodism*, and the editor of *Cornerstones of Spiritual Vitality: Toward an Understanding of Wesleyan Spirituality in Christian Higher Education*.

Jerry Pattengale is university professor at Indiana Wesleyan University, co-director of the Lumen Research Institute, and founding scholar of the Museum of the Bible. He serves on various boards, including Yale University's Jonathan Edwards Center, *Christianity Today*, *Christian*

Scholar's Review, Africa New Life, Changing Destiny, and the National Press Club's Membership Committee. Pattengale holds various distinguished appointments and is the author and editor of numerous books, including *The New Book of Christian Martyrs* (with Johnnie Moore), *The World's Greatest Book: The Story of How the Bible Came to Be* (with Lawrence H. Schiffman), and, most recently, *The Anxious Middle: Planning for the Future of the Christian College* (with Todd C. Ream).

Todd C. Ream is professor of humanities and executive director of faculty research and scholarship at Indiana Wesleyan University, senior fellow for public engagement for the Council for Christian Colleges and Universities, senior fellow for programming for the Lumen Research Institute, and publisher for *Christian Scholar's Review*. He is the author and editor of numerous books, including *Hesburgh of Notre Dame: The Church's Public Intellectual* and, most recently, *The Anxious Middle: Planning for the Future of the Christian College* (with Jerry Pattengale).

Philip Graham Ryken is president and professor of theology at Wheaton College. As Wheaton's eighth president, Ryken advanced the strategic priorities of Deepening Ethnic Diversity, Promoting Liberal Arts Excellence, Enhancing Music and the Performing Arts, and Globalizing a Wheaton Education. He also serves on the board for the Council for Christian Colleges and Universities, The Gospel Coalition, the Lausanne Movement, and the National Association of Evangelicals. Prior to beginning his service at Wheaton in 2010, Ryken served as senior minister of Philadelphia's Tenth Presbyterian Church. He is the author and editor of numerous books, including *When Everything Matters: The Gospel in Ecclesiastes* and, most recently, *Beauty Is Your Destiny: How the Promise of Splendor Changes Everything*.

David I. Smith is professor of education, the founding director of the Kuyers Institute for Christian Teaching and Learning, and the inaugural coordinator of the De Vries Institute for Global Faculty Development at Calvin University. He is the editor of the *International Journal of Christianity and Education* and the author and editor of numerous books, including *Teaching and the Christian Imagination* (with Susan M. Felch) and, most recently, *On Christian Teaching: Practicing Faith in the*

Classroom. Smith is a regular workshop leader on college and university campuses on the relationship shared by faith and teaching. On his own campus, Smith has won the Presidential Award for Exemplary Teaching.

Jessica Hooten Wilson is the Fletcher Jones Chair of Great Books at Pepperdine University's Seaver College of Letters, Arts, and Sciences. A popular speaker and essayist, Wilson is the author or editor of numerous books, including, most recently, *Reading for the Love of God: How to Read as a Spiritual Practice.* Her first book, *Giving the Devil His Due: Demonic Authority in the Fiction of Flannery O'Connor and Fyodor Dostoyevsky,* won *Christianity Today*'s 2018 Book Award for Culture and the Arts. In 2017, Wilson was the recipient of Redeemer University's Emerging Public Intellectual Award.

Amos Yong is professor of theology and mission at Fuller Theological Seminary. He recently completed a term as dean of Fuller's School of Theology and Mission and previously served as faculty member and administrator at Regent University School of Divinity, Bethel University (MN), and Bethany College of the Assemblies of God. Yong is the author or editor of over fifty books and 225 articles. His most recent books include *The Holy Spirit and Higher Education: Renewing the Christian University* (with Dale M. Coulter) and *Renewing the Church by the Spirit: Theological Education After Pentecost.*

GENERAL INDEX